T0301950

An Analysis of

Ferdinand de Saussure's

Course in General Linguistics

Laura E. B. Key
with
Brittany Pheiffer Noble

Published by Macat International Ltd
24:13 Coda Centre, 189 Munster Road, London SW6 6AW.

Distributed exclusively by Routledge
2 Park Square, Milton Park, Abingdon, Oxon OX14 4RN
711 Third Avenue, New York, NY 10017, USA

Routledge is an imprint of the Taylor & Francis Group, an informa business

www.macat.com
info@macat.com

Cataloguing in Publication Data
A catalogue record for this book is available from the British Library.
Library of Congress Cataloguing-in-Publication Data is available upon request.
Cover illustration: Capucine Deslouis

ISBN 978-1-912302-85-7 (hardback)
ISBN 978-1-912127-37-5 (paperback)
ISBN 978-1-912281-73-2 (e-book)

Notice
The information in this book is designed to orientate readers of the work under analysis,
to elucidate and contextualise its key ideas and themes, and to aid in the development
of critical thinking skills. It is not meant to be used, nor should it be used, as a
substitute for original thinking or in place of original writing or research. References and
notes are provided for informational purposes and their presence does not constitute
endorsement of the information or opinions therein. This book is presented solely for
educational purposes. It is sold on the understanding that the publisher is not engaged
to provide any scholarly advice. The publisher has made every effort to ensure that
this book is accurate and up-to-date, but makes no warranties or representations with
regard to the completeness or reliability of the information it contains. The information
and the opinions provided herein are not guaranteed or warranted to produce particular
results and may not be suitable for students of every ability. The publisher shall not be
liable for any loss, damage or disruption arising from any errors or omissions, or from
the use of this book, including, but not limited to, special, incidental, consequential or
other damages caused, or alleged to have been caused, directly or indirectly, by the
information contained within.

CONTENTS

THE MACAT LIBRARY

The Macat Library is a series of unique academic explorations of seminal works in the humanities and social sciences – books and papers that have had a significant and widely recognised impact on their disciplines. It has been created to serve as much more than just a summary of what lies between the covers of a great book. It illuminates and explores the influences on, ideas of, and impact of that book. Our goal is to offer a learning resource that encourages critical thinking and fosters a better, deeper understanding of important ideas.

Each publication is divided into three Sections: Influences, Ideas, and Impact. Each Section has four Modules. These explore every important facet of the work, and the responses to it.

This Section-Module structure makes a Macat Library book easy to use, but it has another important feature. Because each Macat book is written to the same format, it is possible (and encouraged!) to cross-reference multiple Macat books along the same lines of inquiry or research. This allows the reader to open up interesting interdisciplinary pathways.

To further aid your reading, lists of glossary terms and people mentioned are included at the end of this book (these are indicated by an asterisk [*] throughout) – as well as a list of works cited.

Macat has worked with the University of Cambridge to identify the elements of critical thinking and understand the ways in which six different skills combine to enable effective thinking.
Three allow us to fully understand a problem; three more give us the tools to solve it. Together, these six skills make up the **PACIER** model of critical thinking. They are:

ANALYSIS – understanding how an argument is built
EVALUATION – exploring the strengths and weaknesses of an argument
INTERPRETATION – understanding issues of meaning

CREATIVE THINKING – coming up with new ideas and fresh connections
PROBLEM-SOLVING – producing strong solutions
REASONING – creating strong arguments

To find out more, visit **WWW.MACAT.COM.**

CRITICAL THINKING AND *COURSE IN GENERAL LINGUISTICS*

Primary critical thinking skill: INTERPRETATION
Secondary critical thinking skill: REASONING

Ferdinand de Saussure's *Course in General Linguistics* is one of the most influential texts of the 20th-century – an astonishing feat for what is, at heart, a series of deeply technical lectures about the structure of human languages.

What the *Course*'s vast influence shows, fundamentally, is the power of good interpretative skills. The interpretative tasks of laying down and clarifying definitions are often vital to providing the logical framework for all kinds of critical thinking – whether it be solving problems in business, or esoteric academic research. At the time sat which Saussure gave his lectures, linguistics was a scattered and inconsistent field, without a unified method or rigorous approach. He aimed to change that by setting down and clarifying definitions and distinctions that would provide a coherent methodological framework for the study of language. The terms laid down in the *Course* did exactly that – and they still make up the core of linguistic terminology a full century later. More than this, however, Saussure also highlighted the centrality of linguistic interpretation to understanding how we relate to the world, founding "semiotics", or the study of signs – a field whose influence on academics across the humanities and social sciences is unparalleled.

ABOUT THE AUTHOR OF THE ORIGINAL WORK

Ferdinand de Saussure was born in Geneva, Switzerland in 1857, and came from a family of respected scientists. He was a talented linguist and published his first book at the age of 21. Moving beyond traditional methods of studying languages, Saussure dedicated himself to developing a general, universal system to understand how all languages work, but he never published a book on the subject. Instead, he taught a course in general linguistics, and after his death in 1913, a group of his students compiled their notes and published them as a book that went on to redefine linguistics and many other fields of study.

ABOUT THE AUTHORS OF THE ANALYSIS

Dr Laura E. B. Key holds a doctorate in English literature from the University of Manchester. She has taught at Manchester and at the University of Liverpool.

Brittany Pheiffer Noble is a graduate student at Columbia University and holds a Masters degree from Yale University's Divinity School, where she studied religion and theology. Her research focuses on literary and aesthetic theory, alongside theology and history. She is the translator of *Arab Orthodox Christians Under the Ottomans 1516–1831* (2016) and has taught at Sciences Po, Columbia and Dartmouth.

ABOUT MACAT

GREAT WORKS FOR CRITICAL THINKING

Macat is focused on making the ideas of the world's great thinkers accessible and comprehensible to everybody, everywhere, in ways that promote the development of enhanced critical thinking skills.

It works with leading academics from the world's top universities to produce new analyses that focus on the ideas and the impact of the most influential works ever written across a wide variety of academic disciplines. Each of the works that sit at the heart of its growing library is an enduring example of great thinking. But by setting them in context – and looking at the influences that shaped their authors, as well as the responses they provoked – Macat encourages readers to look at these classics and game-changers with fresh eyes. Readers learn to think, engage and challenge their ideas, rather than simply accepting them.

'Macat offers an amazing first-of-its-kind tool for
interdisciplinary learning and research. Its focus on works
that transformed their disciplines and its rigorous approach,
drawing on the world's leading experts and educational institutions,
opens up a world-class education to anyone.'

Andreas Schleicher
Director for Education and Skills, Organisation for Economic
Co-operation and Development

'Macat is taking on some of the major challenges in university
education … They have drawn together a strong team of active
academics who are producing teaching materials that are
novel in the breadth of their approach.'

Prof Lord Broers,
former Vice-Chancellor of the University of Cambridge

'The Macat vision is exceptionally exciting. It focuses
upon new modes of learning which analyse and explain seminal texts
which have profoundly influenced world thinking and so social and
economic development. It promotes the kind of critical thinking
which is essential for any society and economy.
This is the learning of the future.'

Rt Hon Charles Clarke, former UK Secretary of State for Education

'The Macat analyses provide immediate access to the critical
conversation surrounding the books that have shaped their
respective discipline, which will make them an invaluable resource
to all of those, students and teachers, working in the field.'

Professor William Tronzo, University of California at San Diego

WAYS IN TO THE TEXT

KEY POINTS

- Ferdinand de Saussure (1857–1913) was a Swiss linguist—a scholar of the nature and structures of language—whose lectures form the basis of *Course in General Linguistics*.

- *General Linguistics* proposes a "synchronic"* understanding of language (an understanding of how a language works at a fixed point in time rather than a consideration of historical development) and introduces the field of semiotics*—the study of how meaning is communicated through signs.*

- *General Linguistics* changed the landscape of linguistic* studies, marking a clear departure from historical and Neogrammarian schools* of thought ("Neogrammarian" refers to a group of linguists based at the University of Leipzig who focused on discovering the rules of how the sounds of words change).

Who Was Ferdinand de Saussure?

Ferdinand de Saussure, the author of *Course in General Linguistics* (1916), was a linguist and semiotician from Geneva, Switzerland ("linguistics" refers to the study of the nature and constitution of language; "semiotics" is the study of the role signs and symbols play in the communication of meaning). Born in 1857, Saussure's father and great-grandfather were both respected scientists. Saussure was raised in an environment that valued education and professional success. Both family pressure and the competitive culture of Geneva encouraged him to succeed in academia.

Saussure was a high achiever, publishing his first book at the age of 21. He pursued a PhD in Indo-European* languages at the University of Leipzig, after which he went to work at the École Pratique des Hautes Études in Paris. His travels around Europe exposed him to different approaches to linguistics.

Saussure returned to Geneva in 1891 where he completed the research that was to become his most famous work: the *Course in General Linguistics*. This book moved away from a diachronic* style of linguistics (a focus on a language's historical development) towards a synchronic approach (a focus on how a language works as a system at a given point in time). The work was compiled after Saussure's death by fellow linguists (and former pupils) Charles Bally,* Albert Sechehaye,* and Albert Riedlinger,* from lectures given in Geneva between 1906 and 1911. Wade Baskin, a scholar who spent much of his life teaching in Oklahoma and working with Native American languages, first translated the text into English in 1956 as his doctoral dissertation at Teachers College at Columbia University in New York; it has since become world renowned as the key text in the study of the field.

What Does *Course in General Linguistics* Say?

The book documents a university course on general linguistics given three times in the years 1907 to 1911.

Saussure's aims were ambitious: he wanted to change the field of linguistics, believing it to have become a field of scattered methods and interests, lacking scientific rigor and consistency. One goal of the course, then, was to propose a means by which linguistics could be standardized and developed into a more coherent science. To do this,

Saussure argued for a shift from a "diachronic" to a "synchronic" understanding of linguistics. He thought that language should be understood as a set of units that make sense in relation to one another (synchrony) rather than studying language in relation to historical changes and connections (diachrony). For Saussure, all languages are alike since they function in a systemic way. The basic structure of this system is not specific to particular languages; it is only the words, syntax,* and sounds that vary between them.

An important distinction that Saussure makes in *General Linguistics* is between *langue** (language) and *parole** (speaking). For Saussure, language is a fixed structure governed by rules. Individuals experience language passively rather than creatively, as a system that already exists for their use. On the other hand, speaking is the willful and creative activity of the individual. This difference between the stable system of language and the dynamic activity of speaking would become an important and much contested theme in linguistics.

Another aim of the course was to propose that the discipline of linguistics should not only study languages as contained systems, but also examine how language functions in human society. In the first chapter of *General Linguistics*, Saussure states that while there are many different branches of linguistics, none of them has considered language as part of a larger system by which society is governed and understood. How, he asks, does language influence the ways in which people relate to the world?

To answer this question, Saussure offers a discussion of language as a structure made up of signs or symbols (spoken or written words). He then examines how these signs and symbols inform the ways in which people understand and participate in their world. Saussure combines detailed structural analysis with the larger abstract notion that we cannot separate language from thought, or from society. Language is an integral part of the way in which we think about and experience the world. Studying language is part of a wider study of signs, a science that he calls "semiotics." In proposing a new discipline of semiotics, Saussure had an impact far beyond linguistics. His work was referenced, extended, and modified by scholars across the humanities and social sciences.

Why Does *Course in General Linguistics* Matter?

Ferdinand de Saussure's *Course in General Linguistics* revolutionized the study of language by insisting that it should be studied as a complex, closed system. Earlier linguistic studies emphasized history and looked at the tiny details of particular languages from certain times and places, without a consideration of the overarching structure of language. Saussure's approach, doing precisely this, was groundbreaking.

Saussure wanted to show the deep similarities between languages rather than their superficial differences. His approach, called "structural linguistics,"* uses empirical data to prove his claim that all language functions by means of the same basic structure. He offers graphic depictions and key examples to illustrate his theory.

Saussure sees the language system as one of many systems of signs that help society understand and define itself. Saussure concentrated on a theory of language in his text. Yet he predicted that his theory could be used in other areas of study. He was right: the general concept of semiotics has translated well into other disciplines. Semiotics is still recognized as an important way to study human communication, because we use symbols to represent and communicate ideas. A drawing of a tree and the word "tree" are both symbols that represent a certain type of plant. The reason that English speakers use the verbal (spoken) symbol "tree" is because this has been constructed as the symbol to communicate within the system of English. In other languages, the symbol is different—"*arbre*" in French, "árbol" in Spanish, "*baum*" in German, and so on. Saussure called this difference in words, or symbols, "arbitrary," meaning not based on reason. In semiotics, other sign systems, such as body language, visual symbols, or cultural symbols, can also be studied as forms of human interaction. All these systems have a basic structure in common: the individual signs in each system only make sense in relation to the wider system.

General Linguistics has a hugely important place in the study of linguistics. The text has remained influential to this day, and has been translated into many other languages. Since its publication, Saussure's research has reached a wide academic community. It influences disciplines such as anthropology,* sociology,* psychology, literature, cultural studies, history and philosophy, as well as linguistics.

SECTION 1
INFLUENCES

MODULE 1
THE AUTHOR AND THE HISTORICAL CONTEXT

KEY POINTS

- Ferdinand de Saussure's *Course in General Linguistics* revolutionized the way in which linguistics*—the study of the nature and structures of language—was studied and understood.

- Saussure was influenced by comparative linguistics* (the comparison of languages intended to reveal their historical connections) and the Neogrammarian school* (scholars who believed that linguistic changes occur immediately rather than gradually).

- Saussure broke from the historical approach by looking at language synchronically* (as a closed system at a single point in time) and how it relates to society.

Why Read This Text?

Ferdinand de Saussure's *Course in General Linguistics* (1916) is a compilation of lectures given by the Swiss linguist at the University of Geneva between 1907 and 1911 and published after his death. Saussure's work is generally accepted as a groundbreaking movement in the field of modern linguistics.* Saussure argued that language should be understood as a system of signs* that relate to concepts. Importantly, this system of signs is arbitrary: words, for example, do not have an innate relation to the objects and ideas they communicate. There is nothing really similar to a tree about the word "tree."

❝ The great philologists of the nineteenth century studied the history of words and worked out comparisons among languages belonging to a few families… But in order to make this enterprise possible, they had to grant the entities of language—words, roots, conjugation patterns, sound—a persistent identity over time and space. This assumption Saussure was unable to make. The distinction he proposed in the *Course* between diachrony and synchrony was not intended to split linguistics down the middle… but rather to solve a problem that had never been recognized as such or had always been leapt over by faith and intuition. ❞

Perry Meisel, introduction to *Course in General Linguistics*

Saussure's method of focusing on structure is the foundation for semiotics* (the study of how signs and symbols function in culture) and of structural linguistics*—an approach focusing on things such as syntax* (the rules concerning such things as word order in a sentence) that flourished from the early to mid-twentieth century.

Saussure's method of analyzing language was dramatically unlike any that preceded him. Until then, the central focus of linguistic study in Europe had been historical. This means that linguists were primarily interested in how languages changed over time, and how languages were historically related to each other (for example, how Romance languages such as French and Spanish are related to Latin). Instead of examining language by looking at its historical development, Saussure looked at language in its present state. Saussure describes these two different approaches with the terms "diachrony"* (for historical change over time) and "synchrony" (for the present state of language). He analyzed how language functioned as a communicative system made up of verbal and written symbols. He also considered the human element of language: living language is the result of decisions made by individual speakers. The distinction between *langue** (language) and *parole** (speaking) is one of the most iconic contributions Saussure made in his explanation of language as a system.

Saussure's *Course in General Linguistics* has had a large and lasting impact not only on the field of linguistics, but also on the arts and social sciences in general. Saussure's structuralist approach to linguistics—understanding language as a system of signs by which we interpret the world around us—is now generally considered a basic starting point for linguistic study.

Author's Life

Coming from a long line of Swiss scientists, Ferdinand de Saussure was surrounded by academics from his early years. His father, Henri Louis Frédéric de Saussure,* was an entomologist (a scientist who studies insects) and mineralogist (a scientist who studies rocks and minerals); his great-grandfather, Horace-Bénédict de Saussure,* was a prominent physicist and the founder of alpinism (the sport of mountaineering). For generations the family was based in Geneva, the birthplace of the Christian sect of Calvinism,* and was influenced by the Calvinist ideals of hard work and success. It was expected that Saussure would follow his forefathers into academia. He studied ancient languages at the University of Geneva and his first book, *Mémoire sur le Système Primitif des Voyelles dans les Langues Indo-Européennes* (*Memoir on the Primitive System of Vowels in Indo-European Languages*), was published when he was just 21.[1]

After this he traveled to Berlin to continue his studies, focusing on Celtic (a family of language that includes Welsh, Cornish, Irish, and extinct languages of modern-day France and England) and Sanskrit.* Sanskrit, an ancient Indo-European language and the source for modern Hindi (one of the official languages of India), was a rich field for linguists and a popular area of study in nineteenth-century philology* (a branch of linguistics commonly conducted through the study of written language). Saussure would go on to complete his PhD dissertation on the Sanskrit language, "*De l'emploi du génitif absolu en Sanscrit*" ("On the Use of the Genitive* Absolute in Sanskrit"), in 1880. At this stage in his career, Saussure was influenced by comparative linguistics and the Neogrammarian school, both of which took a historical approach to the study of language.

He returned to the University of Geneva in 1891 after he was offered a professorship and worked there for the rest of his life. It was in Geneva, between 1906 and 1911, that he taught the course on general linguistics that was eventually published as the book of the same name. Saussure died in 1913.

Author's Background

Saussure was well placed to undertake his research into linguistics in Germany and Switzerland, as the Germanic countries had become the home of linguistic study during the preceding century. Figures such as Franz Bopp* and August Schleicher* were considered the classic comparative linguists, as scholars who developed comparative approaches to the study of Indo-European languages by looking at similarities and differences between two or more languages over time. These linguists were concerned with the historical development of language, taking an approach known as "diachronic" (from the Greek *dia-* "through" and *chronos* "time"). Out of this work in Germany grew the Neogrammarian school of scholars, who analyzed the effects of society on language change.

Saussure was schooled in classic linguistics by the prominent scholars Georg Curtius* and Ernst Windisch* and, at the University of Leipzig, was taught by one of the leading Neogrammarian linguists, August Leskien.* Saussure modified these approaches to establish his synchronic style of research—a method of research that looked at language as a system. This marked a new direction for linguistic study in the twentieth century.

By calling his approach synchronic (from the Greek *syn–* "together" and *chronos* "time"), Saussure emphasized that he was interested in how language worked at a given moment, not in its historical development. He stressed that the building blocks of language—words and sounds—were arbitrary, which is to say there is no specific inner reason why, for example, English speakers refer to a furry feline animal as a cat—it is just a name that we learn so we can communicate with others. This synchronic approach disproved the idea that language imitates the world around us. Up until Saussure, linguists tended to look at other languages so that they could compare them and track historical change. Saussure wanted to overcome this focus on the separate evolution of individual languages through a consideration of languages as expressions of a common system underlying them all.

NOTES

1   Ferdinand de Saussure, *Mémoire sur le Système Primitif des Voyelles dans les Langues Indo-Européennes* (Leipzig: B. G. Teubner, 1879).

MODULE 2
ACADEMIC CONTEXT

KEY POINTS

- The dominant school of linguistics* at the time, that of the Neogrammarians,* was interested in the social and historical context of languages.

- Linguistics investigated how languages changed over time and in different contexts.

- Saussure wanted to move away from the historical study of languages and instead look at the structure of language as a means of communication.

The Work in its Context

Ferdinand de Saussure's *Course in General Linguistics* moves beyond the work of the Neogrammarian school of linguistics—a school known for its emphasis on diachrony* (the ways in which languages change historically).

Neogrammarians had realized that sound changes in pronunciation—the ways in which the sounds of worlds are altered—happen in a predictable way. This enabled them to reconstruct what dead languages might have once sounded like, based on known phonetic* (pronunciation) rules in living languages.

Neogrammarian scholarship assumed that there was something absolute and standardized about how languages changed over time; the nineteenth-century German linguist Jacob Grimm,* for example, discovered that over time the sound "p" in the Indo-European* languages (a family of languages incorporating languages spoken in Europe and parts of Western, Central, and South Asia) became an "f" in Germanic languages. This is why the word for "foot" begins with

> 66 The comparative school, which had the indisputable merit of opening up a new and fruitful field, did not succeed in setting up the true science of linguistics. It failed to seek out the nature of its object of study. Obviously, without this elementary step, no science can develop a method. 99
>
> Ferdinand de Saussure, *Course in General Linguistics*

"p" in Latin, Greek, and Sanskrit* but begins with an "f" in English, German, and the languages of Scandinavia.[1] Such discoveries were major breakthroughs for the Neogrammarian study of language.

Saussure, however, thought that the work of the Neogrammarians did not go far enough in examining the basic structural principles of all languages. Saussure's contribution to knowledge is to create a general theory of how *all* languages are structured, regardless of their origins or current states. He was looking for principles that explained how language helps humans to think and communicate, not simply principles that explain the form of a specific language, as described by phonology* (the study of the sounds of language).

Saussure wanted to uncover these principles in order to create a bridge between linguistics and other disciplines. He saw a need for categorizing the use of language in the context of the society: "Linguistics is very closely related to other sciences that sometimes borrow from its data, sometimes supply it with data."[2] Saussure's theories partly emerged from his sense that the ideas of linguists had to be categorized and unified.

As Saussure's former pupils Charles Bally* and Albert Sechehaye* noted in their preface to the first edition of *General Linguistics*, Saussure lamented "the dearth of principles and methods that marked linguistics during his developmental period."[3]

Overview of the Field

The German Neogrammarian school of thought was the single most influential movement in linguistics in the early twentieth century. Saussure was influenced by this movement and how it aimed to place comparative linguistic* studies in a historical context. Rather than only look at isolated linguistic examples, the Neogrammarians were beginning to understand language as a system that developed alongside historical and intellectual advances, rather than as an independent sphere with no connections to other disciplines. In particular, August Leskien,* under whom Saussure studied in Leipzig, was a major influence on Saussure. Leskien's argument that language should be understood as a scientific system rather than as a collection of random developments helped to define Saussure's synchronic* approach to language study.

Two other major thinkers in the field were William Dwight Whitney* and Charles Sanders Peirce,* both of whom tried to rethink the ways we understand human language and the relationship of language to reality. Whitney (1827–94) was a well-known American linguist who worked on comparative linguistics with a specialization in Sanskrit, the ancient Indian language of great interest for the Neogrammarians. He had studied with Franz Bopp,* a notable German linguist whose comparative studies in linguistics were the basis for much research on historical linguistics (the historical development of languages).

Charles Sanders Peirce was a versatile thinker who worked on linguistics but focused on logic, mathematics, and semiotics.* At the same time that Whitney and Saussure began to develop universal principles for studying language, Peirce proposed his theory of semiotics—for him this was the relation between any concept and its representation, understood through an analytical method appropriate to the study of words, objects, pictures, actions, and so on.

Section 1: Influences; **Module 2:** Academic Context

Academic Influences

Saussure was trained in the more traditional Neogrammarian approach to studying languages, and he used this methodology in his work. Like the Neogrammarians, his work is sensitive to historical change in languages and the ways in which Indo-European languages relate to each other and evolve over time. But Saussure aimed to move beyond established methodology.

Saussure was not the only thinker breaking with the conventions and methodologies of the Neogrammarians. In developing his general theory of language, Saussure was especially influenced by William Dwight Whitney's[4] *The Life and Growth of Language* (1875),[5] which explored the concept that words have no inherent connection to the concepts or objects they describe.[6] This approach understood language as an evolving system in which meanings are not fixed. Whitney asserted that "every word handed down in every human language is an arbitrary and conventional sign,"* meaning that "any one of the thousand other words current among men … could have been equally well learned and applied to this particular purpose."[7]

In other words, all words in all languages are socially constructed— that is, their meaning depends on shared customs—and have no inherent relationship with the objects or concepts that they describe. There is nothing in a tree that gives it the name "tree" in English, but when English speakers hear the sound "tree" we think of that specific type of plant.

Saussure acknowledges Whitney's recognition that language is a system of signs used by a society for interpretation and communication. He remarks that, according to Whitney, language is a "human institution."[8] He then builds on Whitney's work, introducing the theory of how each sign in a language system consists of both a concept (the "signified")* and a sound image by which the concept is identified (the "signifier").* The signifier and signified translate loosely to the word and the idea to which the word refers.

NOTES

1   Lyle Campbell, *Historical Linguistics* (Cambridge: MIT Press, 1998), 155.

2   Ferdinand de Saussure, *Course in General Linguistics*, ed. Perry Meisel and Haun Saussy, trans. Wade Baskin (New York: Columbia University Press, 2011), 6.

3   Charles Bally and Albert Sechehaye, "Preface to the first edition," in Saussure, *General Linguistics*, liii.

4   John Earl Joseph, *From Whitney to Chomsky: Essays in the History of American Linguistics* (Amsterdam: John Benjamins Publishing Company, 2002), 35.

5   See Saussure, *General Linguistics*, 5.

6   William Dwight Whitney, *The Life and Growth of Language: An Outline of Linguistic Science* (New York: Dover, [1875] 1979).

7   Whitney, *Life and Growth of Language*, 19.

8   John E. Joseph, "The linguistic sign," in *The Cambridge Companion to Saussure*, ed. Carol Sanders (Cambridge: Cambridge University Press, 2004), 59.

13 Søren Kierkegaard, *Concluding Unscientific Postscript to Philosophical*

MODULE 3
THE PROBLEM

KEY POINTS

- During Saussure's time, linguists were interested in charting the development of languages over decades and centuries.

- The historical study of language was concerned with comparative linguistics:* finding common words and grammatical similarities across different languages.

- Saussure wanted to uncover how language worked as a system rather than focusing on comparative linguistics.

Core Question

At the heart of Ferdinand de Saussure's *Course in General Linguistics* are the questions of what all language systems have in common and how language operates as a unified system to produce meaning. These questions are important because most linguistic* studies before Saussure's emphasized the importance of the origins of specific words and meanings—a limited approach that meant that the discipline of linguistics was stuck in a rut, focused only on studying the origins of language.

For Saussure, these origins are unimportant, as each new generation simply accepts the language it inherits without questioning why it is doing so. In other words, the language of the present appears to those who speak it as normal and everyday. In answer to the question of what languages have in common, Saussure proposes that language is a set of arbitrary signs,* and that this set of signs creates and communicates meaning between speakers of the same language.

Saussure's ideas were highly influential on account of their originality. He understood the study of language as part of a larger system of social sciences—an approach lacking in linguistic study at

> ❝ Finally, of what use is linguistics? Very few people have clear ideas on this point, and this is not the place to specify them. But it is evident, for instance, that linguistic questions interest all who work with texts—historians, philologists, etc. Still more obvious is the importance of linguistics to general culture: in the lives of individuals and societies, speech is more important than anything else. ❞
>
> Ferdinand de Saussure, *Course in General Linguistics*

the time. He also developed the concept that words themselves are arbitrary in the sense that there is no fundamental link between the sound, shape, and meaning of a word. Instead, meanings evolve by means of the general consensus of society, which accepts particular words in relation to certain ideas.

The Participants

In the late nineteenth century, linguistics began to emerge as an academic discipline. Its impact was still quite small; only a few universities in Germany offered linguistics and these programs were focused on the comparative study of Indo-European* languages (only a small part of today's field of linguistics), centered on the methodology of the influential linguist Franz Bopp.* Even with figures such as Whitney* in the United States, there was hardly a coherent international conception of the study of language. Saussure's *Course in General Linguistics* arose from what he saw as a lack of consistency in the definition of linguistics as a subject. He was influenced by the Neogrammarian school* of linguistic thought, which focused on historical changes in languages, but saw its limitations and wanted to use it alongside ideas from outside the German language tradition.

Saussure saw that it was important that the field of linguistics was able to explain language in the present rather than the past. He aimed to uncover how the system of language functions as an integral part of the society in which it operates, rather than looking at the history of particular words, phrases, and sounds as previous linguists had done. Because Saussure believed that language reveals how people think, for him understanding present-day language was a way of understanding present-day society.

Although *General Linguistics* is based on Saussure's teachings, he was also impacted by the ideas of his students. The twentieth-century linguist Rudolf Engler* shows how Saussure's relationships and correspondence with his students, especially Antoine Meillet,* Albert Sechehaye,* and Charles Bally,* who prepared the book for publication after Saussure's death, helped him develop and clarify his ideas.[1]

The Contemporary Debate

Saussure explained his ideas in a linguistics program he taught to university students. His research challenged the main principles of linguistic study at the time, breaking with the traditions of the discipline. Saussure's work in Germany, Switzerland, and France during his career led him to challenge the ideas of the academic community around him, creating the new theory of the sign system. This theory, according to which language is a system made up of linguistic signs, was to become the foundation for modern linguistics. Saussure published very little during his lifetime and wrote nothing of theoretical importance. His only publications dealt with language-specific issues in historical linguistics, largely phonology* (the study of language sounds).

Course in General Linguistics was compiled after Saussure's death by his former pupils and fellow linguists Bally, Sechehaye, and Riedlinger,* and was published in 1916. The publication of his work by his former pupils after his death made his work accessible to a global audience, although the fragmentary nature of the evidence that he left behind prevents the reader from having a complete picture of Saussure's exact intentions. Because the book was constructed largely from the lecture notes of his students, the text is heavily influenced by its editors.

Some later scholars, including Saussure scholar Roy Harris,* have questioned whether the text accurately communicates Saussure's understanding of language, which Saussure himself could never explain clearly enough to publish.[2] (Harris examines closely how various scholars have appropriated Saussure's ideas in conflicting ways, noting especially that the discovery of papers written after *General Linguistics* was published casts doubt over the version of his theory elaborated in the book.) Indeed, Saussure struggled to articulate his ideas to the extent that plans for a book never materialized during his lifetime.[3] Despite the potential inaccuracies caused by publishing Saussure's work after his death, using "inevitably approximate"[4] notes by his students, Saussure's ideas are accepted as having been groundbreaking in his field. They paved the way for the development of structuralism* (the theory that language is a system whose various parts only have meaning in relation to the system as a whole) and semiotics* (the study of signs and symbols and their role in the communication of meaning).

NOTES

1   Rudolf Engler, "The Making of *Cours de linguistique générale*," in *The Cambridge Companion to Saussure*, ed. Carol Sanders (Cambridge: Cambridge University Press, 2004), 47–58.

2   See, Roy Harris, *Saussure and His Interpreters* (Edinburgh: Edinburgh University Press, 2003).

3   Perry Meisel and Haun Saussy, "Saussure and His Contexts," introduction to Ferdinand de Saussure, *Course in General Linguistics*, trans. Wade Baskin (New York: Columbia University Press, 2011), xxi.

4   Engler, "Making," 48.

MODULE 4
THE AUTHOR'S CONTRIBUTION

KEY POINTS

- Saussure proposed a three-part system of signs* that could explain the symbolic relation of words to meaning.
- This system revolutionized how linguists approached language.
- The study of systems defined by the relationships between their parts ("systems of relations") became a framework for other disciplines in the sciences and humanities.

Author's Aims

In giving the lectures eventually published as *Course in General Linguistics*, Ferdinand de Saussure's aim was to define the purpose of linguistics* as a subject. He identifies this purpose as deducing (logically proving) "the general laws to which all specific historical [linguistic] phenomena can be reduced."[1] Saussure wanted to elaborate a generally applicable set of rules by which language could be understood. He aimed to research and describe the way in which language functions as a system of meaning. Part of this description of language meant understanding that language is a structure of signs or symbols; understanding language requires examining the symbols used to communicate meaning.

The aims of Saussure's students—the other "authors" of the final manuscript of the *Course in General Linguistics*, as it was based on edited versions of their lecture notes—were to carry on Saussure's ideas and firmly establish a new basis for linguistic study as a discipline.

The book is divided into five sections, each elaborating a different area of linguistic study: part 1 explains what Saussure understands as

> **❝** From whatever direction we approach the question, nowhere do we find the integral object of linguistics. Everywhere we are confronted with a dilemma: if we fix our attention on only one side of each problem, we run the risk of failing to perceive the dualities pointed out above; on the other hand, if we study speech from several viewpoints simultaneously, the object of linguistics appears to us as a confused mass of heterogeneous and unrelated things … There is only one solution to all the foregoing difficulties … we must … use language as the norm of all other manifestations of speech. **❞**
>
> Ferdinand de Saussure, *Course in General Linguistics*

the general principles of linguistics; parts 2 and 3 investigate the differences between synchronic* (looking at language as a system) and diachronic* (looking at change over time) modes of linguistic study; and parts 4 and 5 look at geographical and historical methods of linguistic study. The focus on these different areas seeks to combine existing linguistic research to reveal the gaps in the academic understanding of language. In this way, Saussure aims to uncover the larger patterns shared by all language systems, regardless of historical period or geographical area. This aim is at the heart of Saussure's text.

Approach

The key concept of *Course in General Linguistics* arises from Ferdinand de Saussure's recognition that previous linguists, such as the comparative linguists* and the Neogrammarian school,* were missing an important point: in their attempts to trace the origins of words, they failed to recognize that words themselves have no inherent meaning.

In order to answer the question of how words *do* carry meaning, Saussure looked at how language functions both in society and for the individual, proposing, "If we could embrace the sum of word-images stored in the minds of all individuals, we could identify the social bond that constitutes language."[2]

An important tool for examining this is Saussure's distinction between *langue** and *parole,** ("language" and "speech".) For Saussure, language is a social institution, shared between all members of a society, since "language is not a function of the speaker; it is a product that is passively assimilated by the individual."[3] Language is "both a social product of the faculty of speech and a collection of necessary conventions that have been adopted by a social body to permit individuals to exercise that faculty."[4] Language (*langue*) is individual and social, physical and psychological. On the other hand, speech (*parole*) "is an individual act. It is willful and intellectual."[5]

Saussure sets out to explain how language as a system is flexible and can be used in different ways by any individual. In examining the relationship between the system and the individual, Saussure reveals how humans rely on symbols and systems of signs to make sense of our world and to communicate meaning. Importantly, Saussure emphasizes that language is not the only set of symbols that carry meaning. However, *General Linguistics* is primarily concerned with analyzing language and the interplay between language as an established system (*langue*) and the inventiveness of individual expression (*parole*). Saussure uses examples of everyday language to illustrate his points and also relies on simple graphics to clarify his new concepts and terms.

Contribution in Context

At the time when the *Course in General Linguistics* was first published, in 1916, most linguistic studies focused on philology*—the study of written language, conducted to discover the connections between different languages. Saussure's structuralist* theory of language, according to which language is a system composed of parts whose meaning is decided by their relation to the system as a whole, moves beyond his earlier studies of Indo-European* languages. His first book considered the ways in which vowels change in Indo-European languages; his dissertation was on a grammatical case, the genitive,* in the ancient Indian language of Sanskrit.* These methodologically traditional works established Saussure as a reputable linguist and allowed him to hold various teaching positions. Although he never published again in his lifetime, he left behind manuscripts and notes that have been published after his death. From the work of linguistic scholar Rudolf Engler* we now know that from as early as the 1890s, Saussure was attempting to piece together a system for analyzing language that included the difference between language and speech. Indeed, Engler cites Saussure's initial schema of *langage-langue-parole* in a manuscript now published as "*Ecrits de Linguistique Générale.*"[6]

In analyzing notes taken by students in the course of Saussure's lectures and correspondence in which they discussed his ideas, Engler has shown that Saussure's students were also committed to his project of developing linguistics as a distinct academic discipline and discovering principles that described language as a social institution.[7] This community around Saussure has been called the "Geneva school"* and can be credited with encouraging Saussure to continue working through his theses on language.

While Saussure's ideas as described in his *Course in General Linguistics* are regarded as a revolutionary development in the field of linguistics and semiotics,* in his introduction, Saussure places his study within the existing tradition: "A first impetus was given by the American scholar Whitney,* the author of *Life and Growth of Language* (1875). Shortly afterwards a new school was formed by the neogrammarians (*Junggrammatiker*), whose leaders were all Germans."[8] Whitney argued that language was an institution; earlier scholars had treated it as something beyond human invention (in Saussure's words, language had been wrongly considered a "fourth natural kingdom.")[9] Saussure cites the Neogrammarians as having discovered that language was the product of social forces (in his words, "the collective mind")[10] rather than nature. These discoveries—that language is a man-made institution and the product of collective action—led Saussure to investigate the relationship between individual speakers and the social institution of language.

NOTES

1 Ferdinand de Saussure, *Course in General Linguistics*, ed. Perry Meisel and Haun Saussy, trans. Wade Baskin (New York: Columbia University Press, 2011), 6.

2 Saussure, *General Linguistics*, 13.

3 Saussure, *General Linguistics*, 14.

4 Saussure, *General Linguistics,* 9.

5 Saussure, *General Linguistics*, 9.

6 Rudolf Engler, "The Making of *Cours de linguistique générale*," in *The Cambridge Companion to Saussure*, ed. Carol Sanders (Cambridge: Cambridge University Press, 2004), 48.

7 Engler, "The Making of *Cours de linguistique générale*," 47–58.

8 Saussure, *General Linguistics*, 5.

9 Saussure, *General Linguistics*, 4.

10 Saussure, *General Linguistics*, 5.

SECTION 2
IDEAS

MAIN IDEAS

KEY POINTS

- Saussure proposes that any language can be understood as a semiotic* system—a system of signs;* he stresses that the relationship between signs is what creates meaning in human interactions.

- Saussure argues that signs are arbitrary (that is, there is no real reason why an object is referred to by one word rather than another); their relationships to other signs are the cornerstone of language.

- This thesis was part of Saussure's lectures on linguistics,* published after his death as the *Course in General Linguistics*.

Key Themes

The major themes from Ferdinand de Saussure's *Course in General Linguistics* are:
- Language is a system of signs.
- The signs in language are arbitrary.
- The tripartite (three-part) structure of the linguistic unit
- The distinction between *langue** (language) and *parole** (speaking)

These four major themes all concern how language functions as a structured system that is informed by the relationship between individuals and society. Rather than thinking of language as a closed or finite system, Saussure develops a theory that treats language as living and capable of change. As he says in *General Linguistics*, "Speech always implies both an established system and an evolution; at every moment

> ❝ But what is language [*langue*]? It is not to be confused with human speech [*langage*], of which it is only a definite part ... Speech is many-sided and heterogeneous ... Language, on the contrary, is a self-contained whole and a principle of classification. As soon as we give language first place among the facts of speech, we introduce a natural order into a mass that lends itself to no other classification. ❞
>
> Ferdinand de Saussure, *Course in General Linguistics*

it is an existing institution and a product of the past."[1]

Saussure's work explains how each word functions as part of a larger system of language and how the word makes sense only because of its relationship to other words in that system. This study of a complex of meaningful units existing in relation to each other is what is now called "structuralism."* Even though these units (such as words) carry meaning, their form is arbitrary (there is no inherent reason why in English we use the word "tree" but in Spanish we use the word "árbol" to refer to the same thing.) Once one understands how the general structure of language works, one can analyze any given language as a structure. The way in which the sign system functions can be applied to any language. Moreover, Saussure argues that this science of language has clear structural similarities with other social systems and so his theory could be extended to other disciplines: "A science that studies the life of signs within society is conceivable."[2] This science of signs is called semiotics.*

For Saussure, there are two important dimensions in making language a stable system: the social or collective use of language and the individual's use of language. He calls this distinction *langue* (language) and *parole* (speaking.) Language is a system of signs and speaking is the creative activity of the individual within the confines of this system. There is also a third category, *langage* (speech), which includes the physical dimension of language—how people create and hear auditory signals.

Exploring the Ideas

The text begins with what can be considered Saussure's most important contribution to the subject: his elaboration of the nature of the linguistic sign and the explanation of language as a universal system, regardless of its place or time of origin.

The tripartite (three-part) structure of the linguistic unit is one of Saussure's most widely used contributions to twentieth-century thought. Saussure says that each word consists of the "sign," the "signifier,"* and the "signified."* These three parts make up the unit of speech and its relationship to what is being described.

The signified is the concept to which a word refers; the signifier is the mental image we associate with that concept; the sign is the idea described by the union of these two parts (in Saussure's words: "The two elements [signified and signifier] are intimately united, and each recalls the other.")[3] Illustrations can be found throughout the text to help explain these ideas.

For example, in his lectures, Saussure gives the example of "tree" to help explain his theory. The linguistic sound-image is either the sound "tree" (a word that rhymes with bee), or the image of four letters T-R-E-E. Both these signifiers are connected to a signified, the concept of a large plant with a trunk and branches and leaves. The word "tree" makes one think of a tree and the concept of a tree calls to mind the sound-image "tree." Saussure insists that the use of both the sound "tree" and the image of the word "tree" is arbitrary.

A crucial dimension of Saussure's understanding of linguistic signs is the concept of *value*. Saussure argues that signs have value based on position and relation to other signs. He uses the analogy of chess: the figurine of the king is of no importance outside the game of chess, being simply a small statue; when placed on a chessboard, however, in relation to other pieces with different values such as pawns and queen, it becomes meaningful: we know the value of the king because the piece is surrounded by other pieces that are part of the same game.[4]

The value of a sign gives greater nuance to language, and so, according to Saussure, it also gives greater nuance to human thought (for Saussure, human thought is formed by language—as he puts it, "Without language, thought is a vague, uncharted nebula. There are no preexisting ideas, and nothing is distinct before the appearance of language.")[5] We can look to the adjectives "small," "tiny," "minuscule," and "infinitesimal" to shed some light on the importance of value. These signs (words and concepts) exist relationally and would lose their precise meaning if they could not be compared with similar terms. Because of the link between language and thought, language is not just a representation of reality—it is an important part of reality that helps us understand our existence.

Language and Expression

With the support of his iconic illustrations, Saussure relies on metaphors and analogies to explain his ideas. For example, he uses analogies related to the exchange of money for goods to better describe value, and in discussing the difficult and complex concept of the sign, he discusses different attempts to define it through metaphor: "The two-sided linguistic unit has often been compared with the human person, made up of the body and the soul. The comparison is hardly satisfactory. A better choice would be a chemical compound like water, a combination of hydrogen and oxygen; taken separately, neither element has any of the properties of water."[6]

Saussure's new concepts can appear confusing at first, and Saussure is very aware that his ideas are difficult and sometimes contrary to traditional teaching. Besides his illustrations, he draws on examples from different languages to explain his ideas, and offers long explanations for his new terms and concepts. The material has been presented in a very organized fashion throughout: the entire work is organized by theme and problem, and in each chapter, ideas are organized in an outline.

NOTES

1   Ferdinand de Saussure, *Course in General Linguistics*, ed. Perry Meisel and Haun Saussy, trans. Wade Baskin (New York: Columbia University Press, 2011), 8.

2   Saussure, *General Linguistics*, 16.

3   Saussure, *General Linguistics*, 66.

4   Saussure, *General Linguistics*, 110.

5   Saussure, *General Linguistics*, 112.

6   Saussure, *General Linguistics*, 103.

MODULE 6
SECONDARY IDEAS

KEY POINTS

- Saussure states that changes in language come about when whole groups of people agree to them. He pays attention to geography and syntax* as the organizing principles of language.
- Unlike traditional linguists, Saussure does not attempt to explain all the ways that languages change.
- Saussure's most lasting contribution to the field of linguistics* is in understanding the importance of studying the symbolic relationships between words.

Other Ideas

Ferdinand de Saussure's *Course in General Linguistics* supports its main innovations with important secondary arguments. Careful to show how his study relates to previous historical methodologies that focused on comparative linguistics,* Saussure gives ample evidence and argument for the arbitrary nature of the sign.* He also describes language as a system in order to then explain his theory of the system of signs.

General Linguistics contains a whole chapter on the synchronic* approach to linguistics: that is to say, while it discusses how languages have developed, changed, and coexisted in various countries, the text stresses the important point that specific languages are not innate to speakers living in a particular area or time: "By itself, space cannot influence language."[1] Instead, Saussure highlights the significance of time in generating change. He does this not by focusing on specific reasons for changes in languages that are particular to certain times and

> ❝ Finally, everything that relates to the geographical spreading of languages and dialectal splitting belongs to external linguistics. Doubtless the distinction between internal and external linguistics seems most paradoxical here, since the geographical phenomenon is so closely linked to the existence of any language; but geographical spreading and dialectal splitting do not actually affect the inner organism of an idiom. ❞
>
> Ferdinand de Saussure, *Course in General Linguistics*

places, but by stressing the idea that language change is a result of group acceptance of changes to words, concepts, and ideas.

This collective acceptance of changes is one of the reasons that words are arbitrary. Saussure demonstrates that if words had intrinsic meaning, they would be the same in all languages when, in reality, two words from two different languages but with the same linguistic root often have different meanings. A key example he uses is the distinction between the English "mutton" and the French "*mouton*," one referring to the meat and the other to the animal.[2] For Saussure, distinctions like this prove that words are arbitrary rather than natural.

Saussure shows that language is a system governed by the rules and internal relationships of its parts. For Saussure, language was neither "natural nor rational"[3] and the forms of its internal parts (sound-images) were especially arbitrary compared with other systems (such as gesture or clothing).

Exploring the Ideas

The text's secondary ideas are less clear than the main argument and their lack of clarity has provoked debate over whether or not Saussure saw any merit in sociohistorical approaches to linguistics[4]—approaches founded on a consideration of historical and social contexts.

Saussure's study does not reject historical analysis altogether; the text refers to the importance of more specific studies of certain languages and language groups in terms of understanding how languages have evolved and relate to one another. In moving away from historical studies of language, Saussure tried to emphasize how language changes over time and in different social contexts. Political, economic, or technological changes, for instance, give rise to new words and phrases or alter meanings in a language system. Specifically, these changes take place at the level of the signifier* and the signified,* as part of an exchange between *langue** and *parole.** In Saussure's words, "Language is no longer free, for time will allow the social forces at work on it to carry out their effects. This brings us back to the principle of continuity, which cancels freedom. But continuity necessarily implies change, varying degrees of shifts in the relationship between the signified and the signifier."[5]

By this, Saussure means that language is formed by society—it is not "free" to exist independently from the people who use the language. However, because language changes are not immediate and must happen with the (unconscious) acceptance of society, there is a constantly fluctuating exchange between a language and its speakers.

It has been argued that there is an important connection between the arbitrariness of the sign and Saussure's concept of language as a system. Words are only associated with meanings when members of a society all agree to accept the label given to a concept; even if the rules are arbitrary, speakers intuitively understand them. It should be recognized, however, that, in the words of a Saussure scholar, "language is even more arbitrary than other social institutions, because its rules and various realisations depend on nothing other than itself and its own system."[6] Because the meanings of words and phrases have no fixed ground, the systematic relationships between them become all the more important. People cause languages to further evolve just by using them, and new arbitrary rules spring up on top of the old ones.

Overlooked

Although there is already a wealth of literature on Saussure's *Course in General Linguistics,* later parts of the text have largely been neglected by academic inquiry: the sections on diachronic linguistics* and geographical linguistics. Here, Saussure relates his theory that language should be studied synchronically to existing historical and geographical approaches to linguistics. Many scholars have overlooked this aspect of the text and it could be argued that they have been unjust in criticizing Saussure's lack of attention to sociohistorical context. One such critic is Roman Jakobson,* who modified Saussurean sign theory and applied it to literary study. Although history and geography are certainly not the key elements of Saussure's sign theory, Saussure is careful to mention their relevance.

Scholars pointing to Saussure's omissions have suggested his study is inadequate to its task of offering an overarching linguistic theory. Saussure himself, however, was acutely aware of the limitations of his project and suggests throughout *General Linguistics* that additional work must be done. Moreover, the very fact that Saussure himself did not publish his own theories of language has been used as evidence of Saussure's own dissatisfaction with the comprehensiveness of his ideas. In this sense, he may have been in agreement with his critics.

His work has also been criticized, for example by the scholar Jonathan Culler,* for ignoring matters of syntax (the rules governing things such as word order) and parts of speech.[7] First, Saussure does in fact discuss syntax; admittedly not in detail, but he stresses that syntax forms only part of a system of grammatical rules. Saussure attempted to head off criticism by warning that he deliberately avoided detailed discussions of grammar because he wanted to outline a general theory: "I cannot undertake that task here, for my aim is limited to stating only the most general principles."[8]

Before the translation of his work into English in 1959, Saussure had almost no impact on English-speaking studies of language. With the 1996 discovery of copious notes by Saussure, there was renewed interest in his work as researchers compared the text with these new materials. For present-day readers, then, there is little in *General Linguistics* that has not been subject to academic scrutiny.

NOTES

1   Ferdinand de Saussure, *Course in General Linguistics*, ed. Perry Meisel and Haun Saussy, trans. Wade Baskin (New York: Columbia University Press, 2011), 198.

2   Saussure, *General Linguistics*, 115–6.

3   Claudine Normand, "System, arbitrariness, value," in *The Cambridge Companion to Saussure*, ed. Carol Sanders (Cambridge: Cambridge University Press, 2004), 88.

4   See Sanders, *Cambridge Companion to Saussure*.

5   Saussure, *General Linguistics*, 78.

6   Normand, "System, arbitrariness, value," 88.

7   See, Jonathan Culler, *Ferdinand de Saussure* (New York: Penguin Books, 1977).

8   Saussure, *General Linguistics*, 137.

MODULE 7
ACHIEVEMENT

KEY POINTS

- *General Linguistics* successfully revolutionized the field of linguistics* and formed the basis for broader studies of signs* in literature and culture.

- The text exists thanks to the work of Saussure's students, who collected, edited, and published the notes on his lectures.

- Since *General Linguistics* was published after his death, Saussure could neither clarify ideas that seemed undeveloped, nor respond to criticisms.

Assessing the Argument

Ferdinand de Saussure's *Course in General Linguistics* offers a general theory, applicable to every language, of how language operates as a system of signs mediating between people and ideas. Rather than tracing the connections between particular words, phrases, and sounds, he looks at the methods by which arbitrary words become linked to specific concepts, and how these words become connected to form a complete language system. Saussure thus moves away from the small details of etymology* (the study of word origins) and phonology* (the study of sounds in a language) in favor of a universal linguistic framework.

Saussure believed that his project was necessary to unify linguistics as a discipline. While the effects of his *Course in General Linguistics* were not immediate, within 20 years the text had revolutionized linguistic study. Existing linguistic studies of Saussure's time tended to be specialized—looking at a particular language or group of languages in a specific context—instead of working toward a general, coherent

> ❝ Semiology would show what constitutes signs, what laws govern them. Since the science does not yet exist, no one can say what it would be; but it has a right to existence, a place staked out in advance. Linguistics is only a part of the general science of semiology; the laws discovered by semiology will be applicable to linguistics. ❞
>
> Ferdinand de Saussure, *Course in General Linguistics*

science of linguistics. The *Course in General Linguistics* managed to fulfill this purpose, following Saussure's proclamation that linguistics forms part of a larger field of study: semiotics.*[1] In the decades following the publication of Saussure's work, a branch of scientific study named semiotics did emerge, and Saussure is considered the pioneer of this field. Saussure's ideas first gained attention thanks to the efforts of his students, especially Albert Sechehaye,* who not only edited the text but also wrote about Saussure's ideas in the 1910s.[2] (As Christian Peuch writes, "Sechehaye deserves all the more credit because it took many years for the importance of the semiological status of *langue** to become apparent to the readers of the *Cours*, although after the Second World War Saussure would appear essentially as the originator of what Roland Barthes* called 'the adventure of semiology'.*")[3] In the 1920s, Saussure's ideas became important to Slavic linguists and then spread throughout Europe and into America after World War II.* It was especially in the mid-twentieth century that people working outside of linguistics began to see the usefulness of semiotics.

Achievement in Context

In some ways, the text contradicts itself by prioritizing a synchronic* approach to language study (approaching language as a system) but spending a significant portion of the book discussing diachronic* (or historical) methods. In particular, the focus on the synchronic in Saussure's introduction seems to contradict some parts of the text that follow, which includes historical and geographical consideration of language development. Perhaps this apparent contradiction is present because the book was put together and published after Saussure's death, by his former students. It is made up of an edited collection of lecture notes, and as a whole the book seeks to give a historical and geographical overview of linguistics while at the same time championing a new approach that emphasizes other aspects of language.

The editors wanted *General Linguistics* to act as a guide to the scholarly history of the discipline and to elaborate Saussure's own theories. While the book has become world renowned for the groundbreaking nature of Saussure's ideas, the wealth of historical and philological* details emphasize Saussure's mastery of traditional linguistics ("philological" here referring to the study of written languages in order to discover links between them). This allowed him to look beyond familiar methods while still providing concrete examples from over a dozen languages to prove the usefulness of his synchronic theory.

Saussure's ideas were obviously a success in the context of their original purpose as a series of lectures because they inspired his students to publish and share them. Had Saussure been able to publish *General Linguistics* during his lifetime, it is possible that it would have enjoyed more immediate popularity thanks to his highly-regarded position as a leading linguist. In reality, Saussure's work had an unusual route to publication, and it is remarkable that he is now famous for ideas that he shared with only a small group of people.

Limitations

Saussure believed that one could "determine the forces that are permanently and universally at work in all languages."[4] Such claims about the universal applicability of his theory to language were seriously challenged in the twentieth century. His attempts at uncovering abstract principles explaining all language have been criticized as characteristic of his time and reminiscent of European idealism*—a philosophical approach holding that reality is created by the human mind and must be understood through a consideration of things such as the nature of thought, perception, and so on. The quest for universal forces at work in all languages is related to the conviction of the Neogrammarian school* that all Indo-European* languages share semantic (meaning-related) and grammatical forms that are masked by phonological change (that is, changes in how words are spoken.)

Saussure's insistence on the stability and superiority of written language over spoken language has been critiqued by the French literary theorist Jacques Derrida* as a form of conservatism common to his age.[5] On the other hand, linguists such as Noam Chomsky*— while not a follower of Saussure—argued that grammar is universal, being hard-wired into the human brain. While different from Saussure's search for a universal system, Chomsky's theory illustrates that the search for universal principles in linguistics is not only a late nineteenth-century phenomenon.

Saussure's teachings have been criticized for failing to take into account all the different functions of language and the variety of social forces acting on language. For instance, the Russian linguist Roman Jakobson* rejects Saussure's metaphor of language as a game-like system, and instead argues for six major functions of language.[6] Two other Russian linguists, Mikhail Bakhtin* and Valentin Vološinov,* both criticize Saussure's assumption that language can be understood through such objective analysis, arguing that it must be interpreted in the context of the historical period and society in which it is used.

NOTES

1   Ferdinand de Saussure, *Course in General Linguistics*, ed. Perry Meisel and Haun Saussy, trans. Wade Baskin (New York: Columbia University Press, 2011), 16.

2   Christian Puech, "Saussure and structuralist linguistics in Europe," in *The Cambridge Companion to Saussure*, ed. Carol Sanders (Cambridge: Cambridge University Press, 2004), 124–38.

3   Puech, "Saussure and structuralist linguistics," 126.

4   Saussure, *General Linguistics*, 6.

5   Geoffrey Bennington, "Saussure and Derrida," in *Cambridge Companion to Saussure*, 189.

6   Stephen C. Hutchings, "The Russian critique of Saussure," in *Cambridge Companion to Saussure,* 147.

MODULE 8
PLACE IN THE AUTHOR'S WORK

KEY POINTS

- Saussure created a study of linguistics* that moved beyond historical, comparative, or Neogrammarian* approaches.

- Based on lectures given in the final years before his death, *General Linguistics* represents the work of a mature thinker.

- *General Linguistics* is the defining work of Saussure's career, even though his students compiled and published it after he died.

Positioning

Ferdinand de Saussure's *Course in General Linguistics* offers an account of his thought in the period before his death. In his earlier years, he was most interested in the analysis of particular languages and language systems such as Greek, Latin, Germanic languages, and the extinct ancient Indian language of Sanskrit,* and it was these languages that his earlier teaching focused on.[1] Saussure published little in his lifetime; he wrote brief articles for linguistics publications and only a single book, on vowel systems in Indo-European* languages. Published when he was just 21, it cemented Saussure's reputation as an exceptional thinker.[2] Indeed, one scholar explains that "one of the greatest French linguists, Antoine Meillet,* later on called it the most beautiful book of comparative grammar ever written," adding "the judgment is still valid."[3] During his time teaching in Paris, Saussure became a Knight of the French Legion of Honor* (a title granted by the French state for exceptional service or merit).[4] After leaving Paris for Geneva, he was recognized by the Linguistic Society of Paris for his important work on Indo-European vowels.[5]

❝ Anyone who confronts the complex object that is language so as to make a study of it will necessarily approach this object from one side or another, which will never be the whole of language—even assuming that it is well chosen. **❞**

Ferdinand de Saussure, *Writings in General Linguistics*

In short, despite publishing very little, Saussure was well known in the small community of linguists in France, Switzerland, and Germany as a great linguist. Published after his death, *Course in General Linguistics* summarizes the theories Saussure developed in the later stages of his career.

Saussure is now credited with having successfully reconstructed parts of Indo-European phonology* (the sounds of spoken language), based on his knowledge of how languages evolve. His theory reconstructed the vowels of the ancestral language from which modern Indo-European languages originate through a system akin to ablaut* (a form of change in vowels). He used the term "laryngeals"* to describe these changed vowel sounds. His theory, first proposed in 1879, was proved true after the discovery of Hittite* texts in the early twentieth century. (Hittite was a language spoken in present-day Syria and southern Turkey in the sixteenth to thirteenth centuries B.C.E.). Saussure was not, however, widely credited for his discovery until 1935, when the Polish linguist Jerzy Kuryłowicz published an article on his theory.[6]

When it came to the study of Indo-European vowel sounds, Saussure's project of reconstruction fell well inside the established field of nineteenth-century linguistics and its concern for lost historical forms. But his ability to develop structures for analyzing language effective enough to make predictions about missing information offers an indication of his intellectual ability. This ability found expression in his later theories regarding language as a system of values and a series of related signs*—a system that can only be understood through the relationships between elements inside it.

The linguists Rudolf Engler* and Simon Bouquet's* book *Writings in General Linguistics* emphasizes the need to analyze Saussure's whole body of work rather than just *General Linguistics*, stressing that Saussure's theory "is to be found in three groups of texts": in his own writings, in the notes of his students, and in the *General Linguistics*, compiled by Charles Bally* and Albert Sechehaye* after Saussure's death.[7] For Engler and Bouquet, it is important to understand Saussure's ideas as unfinished.

Integration

Saussure began to write a book on general linguistics during his lifetime, but abandoned the project. Although his notebooks from this attempt have since been found and published, *General Linguistics* remains Saussure's most famous and widely cited text. He is much better known for his general theories of language than his contributions to historical linguistics.

Much of Saussure's previous teaching and research focused on etymology and sound change. Moving away from this historical approach to linguistics, *General Linguistics* offers a more thorough and comprehensive style of linguistic study, suggesting that a general theory of language can be applied across countries and cultures (as opposed to being applicable to only one language, such as Sanskrit). While the text is very much recognized as the work of Saussure, it is based on the notes of many students taken over multiple years. As such, it has inspired debate about how accurately it reflects the entirety of Saussure's thought.

In 1996, unfinished writings of Saussure were discovered, now published in English as *Writings in General Linguistics*. These writings expand on themes from the *Course in General Linguistics*, especially because they also include Saussure's lecture notes. They also reveal that Saussure was always very cautious and nuanced in discussing binaries—concepts with opposing poles, such as "light" and "dark". As binaries would go on to become a major organizing principle in structuralism,* we can see that Saussure was conscious of both their descriptive power and their conceptual shortcomings.[8] For example, Saussure recognized the problematic—but necessary—distinction between language and speaking, and to address this he offered a variety of examples, metaphors, and explanations to try to work out their exact relationship.

Significance

Saussure's core insight was that language was one of a number of systems of signs. All these systems taken together form a larger science of signs that allows ideas to be expressed. These are the mechanisms through which meaning is shared throughout a society. Other examples of such sign systems that he offers are "symbolic rites, polite formulas [and] military signals."[9] The study of these systems was named "semiology"* by Saussure, a term now interchangeable with "semiotics."*

The unfinished nature of Saussure's work has led to many varying interpretations of what he meant to say, and debates about these different ideas continue to this day.[10] The scholars Perry Meisel* and Haun Saussy* note that the published text by Charles Bally, Albert Sechehaye, and Albert Riedlinger* differs from other students' accounts of Saussure's lecture series: "[They] designed the published course to foreground the analysis of linguistic 'system,' the synchronic* representation of what Saussure called '*langue*'* … But when Saussure taught his course, he put its stresses differently."[11]

Regardless of academic disputes about *General Linguistics*, there is no doubt that the work is a seminal contribution to twentieth-century thought. As the eminent Saussure scholar Carol Sanders* remarks:"At the turn of the nineteenth and twentieth centuries, general linguistics, as a discipline that examines how language works and how best to describe the current state of a living language (as opposed to tracing the history of past language states), was barely constituted; Saussure was one of the main thinkers who contributed to establishing the principles of the discipline as we know it today."[12]

NOTES

1   See Perry Meisel and Haun Saussy, "Saussure and His Contexts," introduction to Ferdinand de Saussure, *Course in General Linguistics*, trans. Wade Baskin (New York: Columbia University Press, 2011), xx.

2   Ferdinand de Saussure, *Mémoire Sur Le Système Primitif des Voyelles dans les Langues Indo-Européennes* (Leipzig: B. G. Teubner, 1879).

3   Anna Morpurgo Davies, "Saussure and Indo-European linguistics," in *The Cambridge Companion to Saussure*, ed. Carol Sanders (Cambridge: Cambridge University Press, 2004), 15.

4   See John E. Joseph, *Saussure* (Oxford: Oxford University Press, 2012), 373.

5   Davies, "Saussure and Indo-European linguistics," 9.

6   See Jerzy Kuryłowicz, Études indoeuropéennes I (*Indo-European Studies* I), 1935.

7   Ferdinand de Saussure, *Writings in General Linguistics*, ed. Simon Bouquet and Rudolf Engler, trans. Carol Sanders and Matthew Pires (Oxford: Oxford University Press, 2006), xi.

8   Saussure, *Writings in General Linguistics*, xxi.

9   Saussure, *Course in General Linguistics*, 16.

10 See, for example, Paul Bouissac, *Saussure: A Guide for the Perplexed* (New York: Continuum, 2010) and Roy Harris, *Saussure and His Interpreters* (Edinburgh: Edinburgh University Press, 2003).

11 Meisel and Saussy, "Saussure and His Contexts," xxv.

12 Carol Sanders, "Introduction: Saussure today," in *Cambridge Companion to Saussure*, 1.

SECTION 3
IMPACT

MODULE 9
THE FIRST RESPONSES

KEY POINTS

- *General Linguistics* was criticized for being too general and lacking in the type of philological* precision (precision in the study of written language) or historical analysis that had, until then, defined the study of linguistics.*
- The text was largely a success, and despite criticisms, became enormously influential.
- The translation of the text into English in 1959 inspired new interest in Saussure, some 40 years after his death.

Criticism

As Ferdinand de Saussure's *Course in General Linguistics* was not available in English translation until 1959, the bulk of criticism from the book's publication in 1916 up until then came from non-Anglophone European scholars. Since the text's initial publication, readers have had mixed opinions as to the universal applicability of Saussure's science of signs.* The Russian linguists Valentin Vološinov* and Roman Jakobson* saw the text as too generalized, ignoring the nuances of particular sign systems and contexts. Vološinov and Mikhail Bakhtin* criticized Saussure in the 1920s, accusing Saussure of formalism.* In brief, this means that they thought that Saussure's concept of language as a closed (or formal) system ignored the vital role of human creativity, dialogue, and agency in communication.[1]

Roman Jakobson used Saussure's work to help him develop many of his own, different ideas about the nature of the linguistic sign and the system of language. Jakobson disagreed with Saussure's binary* of *langue*/*parole** and instead created his own binary of code/message.

❝ The fact remains that, although Saussure's ideas have made great headway, semiology* remains a tentative science. The reason for this may well be simple. Saussure, followed in this by the main semiologists, thought that linguistics merely formed a part of the general science of signs. Now it is far from certain that in the social life of today there are to be found any extensive systems of signs outside human language. ❞

Roland Barthes, *Elements of Semiology*

The term "code" is meant to imply that there are multiple distinct goals in speaking, whereas for Saussure language is an abstract system with the single purpose of communication. Jakobson proposed that any study of language would have to classify the different uses of language in order to arrive at meaningful rules, beyond Saussure's idea that language exists only to communicate meaning. Jakobson identifies six functions of language in his own structuralist* analysis: poetic, referential, emotive, conative, phatic, and metalingual.[2] "Conative" denotes language indicating an attempt to perform an action ("She reached for the biscuits," for example); "phatic" denotes language whose purpose has more to do with social interaction than the communication of meaning ("Well I never," for example, or "What's up?"); "metalingual" simply means language used to discuss language ("verb," "phatic," and "metalingual" itself are all examples).

The Saussure scholar Roy Harris* wrote a book on the topic of how Saussure's work was received, showing how his ideas were accepted, adopted, or reworked by major twentieth-century figures including the linguists Leonard Bloomfield,* Louis Hjelmslev,* and Noam Chomsky,* and theorists Claude Lévi-Strauss,* Roland Barthes,* and Jacques Derrida.*[3] For all of them, Saussure's ideas about language as a system and the complex nature of the sign offered something important to linguistics, semiotics,* literary analysis, or critical theory* (an analysis of culture commonly conducted on political lines). Other theorists, however, fine-tuned his theories so that they could use them in their own work.

Responses

As *General Linguistics* was published after Saussure's death, the role of responding to the text fell to its editors, Charles Bally,* Albert Sechehaye,* and Albert Riedlinger.* Bally and his colleagues edited only the first edition and so they never directly respond to the debates that arose after the publication of the book. Bally and Riedlinger went on with their own careers and did not try to represent Saussure's theories and positions.

Because Saussure was well known in his lifetime for his work on historical linguistics, *General Linguistics* appeared to early readers as a distortion of Saussure's legacy, because it broke with this tradition.[4] Sechehaye, however, wrote a long review of the text in 1917, the year after it was published, praising it for its important new concepts and terminology for linguistics and psychology (a field, dealing with the human mind and behavior, in which Sechehaye was also trained.)[5] This review was not a response to specific criticism, but an attempt to head off any potential resistance to Saussure's project. Sechehaye's endorsement of Saussure's text not only helped to defend Saussure's claims, but also to promote Saussure as a philosophical thinker capable of dealing with abstract questions.[6]

Over the next decade, *General Linguistics* gradually gained a wider audience. It became popular with linguists and others in different parts of Europe, such as the communities of linguists in Paris and Prague who shared close professional ties. When the first international congress of linguistics took place in 1928, "the *CLG* [*Course in General Linguistics*] was seen as the main starting point for innovation in linguistics."[7] Since then, other critical editions of the text have appeared in its original French and a number of other languages, including German, Japanese, Spanish, and English. Not only did the text appear after Saussure's death, but since some of its key translations didn't appear until after the editors had also died (both Sechehaye and Bally died in the late 1940s), the text has enjoyed an important presence in Western thought without either its author or any of its editors being alive to respond directly to criticisms.

Conflict and Consensus

Today, Saussure's text is widely understood as having been groundbreaking in its contemporary context. It revolutionized the way language was studied by offering a general definition of what linguistics is and how it should be approached. Saussure is now considered one of the founders of structuralism—a school of thought that approaches language as a structure whose parts can be understood by a consideration of how they relate to each other. Structuralism began as a way to analyze languages, and was later used by people analyzing literary texts and other forms of cultural production. At the heart of structuralism is the idea—first expressed by Saussure—that language is constructed by societies, rather than arising directly from nature. While other structuralists such as Roman Jakobson expanded Saussure's claims by introducing categories of language, for example, Saussure's main ideas were foundational to the field of modern linguistics.

The question remains as to which version of Saussure's linguistic theory is the definitive one, partly a result of the text being published after Saussure's death and edited by his former students. The debate was fueled by the discovery of Saussure's unpublished papers, which have since been published. Many Saussure scholars over the past century have tried to answer the question of what Saussure's theory really meant through the publication of critical editions, new-found notes, and manuscript materials. In the English-speaking world, the most prominent of these scholars are Simon Bouquet,* Rudolf Engler,* Roy Harris, and Eisuke Komatsu,* all of whom have collaborated on major new editions of material by Saussure.[8]

The notion of language as a sign system remains Saussure's greatest contribution to linguistics. It has become fundamental to the study of linguistics, to the point that it no longer merits question. The field of semiotics, invented by Saussure, grew dramatically in the twentieth century, influencing not just linguistics, but critical theory, art history, anthropology* (the study of human beings, commonly conducted through the analysis of societies and cultures), and cultural studies (inquiry into cultural behavior, conducted through a number of different political approaches, and drawing on the wider aims and methods of fields as diverse as history, literary theory, film studies, and political theory).

NOTES

1 Michael Holquist, *Dialogism: Bakhtin and His World* (London: Routledge, 2002) 42–68.

2 Roman Jakobson, "Linguistics and Poetics," in *Style in Language* (Cambridge, MA: MIT Press, 1960), 350–77.

3 Roy Harris, *Saussure and his Interpreters* (Edinburgh: Edinburgh University Press, 2003).

4 Christian Puech, "Saussure and structuralist linguistics in Europe," in *The Cambridge Companion to Saussure*, ed. Carol Sanders (Cambridge: Cambridge University Press, 2004), 125.

5 Albert Sechehaye, "Les problèmes de la langue à la lumière d'une théorie nouvelle," *Revue Philosophique de la France et de l'Etranger* 84 (1917), 1–30.

6 Sechehaye, "Les problèmes de la langue," 8.

7 Peuch, "Saussure and structuralist linguistics," 126.

8 See, Ferdinand de Saussure, *Writings in General Linguistics*, ed. Simon Bouquet and Rudolf Engler, trans. Carol Sanders and Matthew Pires (Oxford: Oxford University Press, 2006), and Ferdinand de Saussure, *Third Course of Lectures on General Linguistics (1910–1911)*, ed. and trans. Roy Harris and Eisuke Komatsu (Oxford: Pergamon Press, 1993).

MODULE 10
THE EVOLVING DEBATE

KEY POINTS

- Saussure's text made a great impact in the field of linguistics,* establishing a new study of language and culture: semiotics.*

- Saussure's lectures provided the basis for structuralism,* one of the most important intellectual frameworks in the twentieth century; later schools of thought such as poststructuralism*—an approach to cultural analysis that questions the possibility of the objective account—are indebted to it.

- Saussure's ideas about semiotics transformed how people understood language, making it possible to see it as a system of communication rather than a product of the historical development of grammar and words, opening up new ways of analyzing books, films, and so on.

Uses and Problems

Ferdinand de Saussure's *Course in General Linguistics* completely revolutionized the field of linguistics, establishing an overall framework for a discipline that had previously been fragmentary. By introducing a general set of rules that linguists should apply to the study of language, Saussure inspired the development not only of structural* linguistics, but also of semiology,* or semiotics, as it came to be known (the study of meaning in general). Structuralism and semiotics would become important schools of thought in the twentieth century, thus carrying Saussure's ideas about sign,* signifier,* and signified* into various fields of the humanities and social sciences.

> ❝ We are aware of our responsibility to our critics. We are also aware of our responsibility to the author, who probably would not have authorized the publication of these pages. This responsibility we accept wholly, and we would willingly bear it alone. Will the critics be able to distinguish between the teacher and his interpreters? We would be grateful to them if they would direct toward us the blows which it would be unjust to heap upon one whose memory is dear to us. ❞

Charles Bally and Albert Sechehaye, preface to Ferdinand de Saussure, *Course in General Linguistics*

The novelty of Saussure's theory of the sign as part of a universal language system that is relevant to all languages meant that many readers paid little attention to the historical and geographical aspects of the book. Most studies focus on part 1 of the book, in which Saussure's general theory of the sign is explained, and say little or nothing about the other four sections of the text. As a result, some scholars have tried to redress the balance in recent years. Simon Bouquet* and Rudolf Engler's* publication of Saussure's papers in 2002, for example, presents a collection of Saussure's previously unpublished manuscripts and notes that can be read alongside the *Course in General Linguistics*, and their book aims to separate the myths around Saussure's work from his original ideas.[1] The new materials added to Saussure's body of work have ensured that debates about his output have continued throughout the decades and various interpretations of his work now constitute a whole subject in themselves.

Schools of Thought

Saussure's work has had a wide and lasting impact on the study of linguistics, inspiring debate about the nature of representation and the ways in which society is governed by a system of signs. The rise of structuralism (the theory that language is a system whose parts only have meaning in relation to the whole) owes much to Saussure. Alongside Saussure, linguists Roman Jakobson* and Nikolai Trubetskoy* helped to introduce structuralism as an important approach in linguistics and literary studies.

The development of poststructuralism in the 1960s and 1970s posed a challenge, however, to the thought inspired by Saussure. Poststructuralism challenged the idea that human language or literature could be studied as closed systems or structures. Instead, poststructuralism insisted that outside factors—culture, history, the reader's own personal subjectivity—crucially shape language and literary texts. Poststructuralist critiques of Saussure have some similarities with Mikhail Bakhtin's* accusations that Saussure's method ignores individual creativity or cultural forces.

Thinkers such as the French anthropologist* Claude Lévi-Strauss* and the Italian literary theorist Umberto Eco* have developed semiotic approaches to philosophy and anthropology to study how symbols work in specific contexts. They show how kinship (family) relations and cultural traditions such as rituals or myths are complex symbolic systems that demonstrate the values, fears, and beliefs of societies, in ways that are illuminated by semiotic analysis.

In their introduction to the latest edition of *General Linguistics*, the editors claim, "The philosophical consequences of Saussure's inventiveness are more indirect and profound than they are programmatic [planned]. Roland Barthes,* Michel Foucault,* Jacques Derrida,* and Jacques Lacan* are the surest proofs."[2] Barthes expanded Saussure's system, using semiotics to analyze images, ideologies, and rituals. Barthes and Foucault are both concerned with power and how it shapes systems of communication and knowledge. Derrida, an iconic poststructuralist philosopher, challenges the idea that clear structural relationships between two things are possible, by arguing that language in fact produces meaning in an unstable way. Lacan's work, particularly regarding symbols, was especially inspired by an exploration of the relationship between ideas derived from the work of the founder of psychoanalysis,* the Austrian thinker and neurologist Sigmund Freud,* and semiotics.

In Current Scholarship

Recent work on Ferdinand de Saussure's *Course in General Linguistics* has reinterpreted the original book in the light of papers and manuscripts by Saussure discovered in the last 20 years. Simon Bouquet and Rudolf Engler's publication of Saussure's papers in 2006, for example, aims to distinguish the myths about Saussure's work from his original ideas.[3]

The latest edition of the linguist Roy Harris's* *Saussure and His Interpreters* argues that, over time, Saussure's critics have lost sight of his ideas because they have been influenced by the many differing interpretations of his work.[4] For instance, Harris argues that Saussure's ideas are far more dependent on historical factors than previously thought and have one foot in traditional nineteenth-century philology.* This argument portrays Saussure as an original and innovative thinker, but neither unorthodox nor careless in his methodology or findings.

Other scholars are interested in how Saussure's traditional training in comparative linguistics* actually gave rise to his new perspectives on language. Still others, such as Perry Meisel* and Haun Saussy,* are interested in how the "medieval saint or hero" figure that Saussure is now seen as, functions entirely separately from Saussure as an actual person.[5] Work on Saussure remains diverse, rather than being united by one framework or voice.

Scholars such as Dirk Baecker* and Niklas Luhmann* have used sign theory to unite sociology* (the study of society and social behavior) and mathematics, indicating the continued relevance of a science of signs in the modern era. Luhmann attempts to reconcile binary* systems of reference—common in systems theory, a field based on the mathematical study of systems—with the tripartite (three-part) system of meaning founded on sign, signifier, and signified that Saussure proposed.[6] Luhmann maintains that all social systems are communication systems, with human society being the largest system of them all. His analysis of social systems takes into consideration how seemingly closed systems actually interact and influence each other, an idea that goes beyond Saussure's initial description of language as a system.[7]

NOTES

1 Ferdinand de Saussure, *Writings in General Linguistics*, ed. Simon Bouquet and Rudolf Engler, trans. Carol Sanders and Matthew Pires (Oxford: Oxford University Press, 2006).

2 Ferdinand de Saussure, *Course in General Linguistics*, ed. Perry Meisel and Haun Saussy, trans. Wade Baskin (New York: Columbia University Press, 2011), xvi.

3 See, Saussure, *Writings in General Linguistics*.

4 Roy Harris, *Saussure and His Interpreters* (Edinburgh: Edinburgh University Press, 2003).

5 Saussure, *General Linguistics*, xxii.

6 Dirk Baecker, ed., *Problems of Form*, trans. Michael Irmscher and Leah Edwards (Stanford, CA: Stanford University Press, 1999); Niklas Luhmann, "'Sign as Form'—A Comment," *Cybernetics and Human Knowing* 6, no.3 (1999): 39–46.

7 Robert C. Holub, *Jurgen Habermas: Critic in the Public Sphere* (London: Routledge, 2006), 114.

MODULE 11
IMPACT AND INFLUENCE TODAY

KEY POINTS

- Saussure's *Course in General Linguistics* is compulsory reading for any student of linguistics* or semiotic* studies.

- While Saussure proposes that his system of signs* can be applied to any system of communication, scholars find that some fields are more suitable for semiotic analysis than others.

- The much more recent publication of Saussure's *Writings on General Linguistics* shows that Saussure had in fact a nuanced balance of synchrony* (study based on language as a present system) and diachrony* (language studied through its historical development) in his theory.

Position

Ferdinand de Saussure's *Course in General Linguistics* made language central to the study of how signs work in society. He believed that language is the "most important" of all sign systems because it is our key form of communication.[1] The study of sign systems that Saussure outlined through his theory of general linguistics has been expanded to include a multitude of areas of study: psychological signs, historical signs, anthropological* signs, to name just a few. The application of Saussure's theories to these fields has created new ways of understanding human culture and society.

For example, the French semiotician Roland Barthes's* analysis of "myths," a word he uses to refer to everyday conventions, was heavily influenced by Saussure's ideas. Just as Saussure saw language as a human-made system of arbitrary signs—that is, a network of related

❝ Coming forward towards the present day, we have stopped short of Frege, Russell and Wittgenstein, and of the post-Saussurean descriptive linguists, because their work marks the adoption of new frameworks of linguistic inquiry, rather than a continuation of the traditional one. Saussure we have taken as our *terminus ad quem* [destination] because he makes the break with the old tradition so consciously and so emphatically. ❞

Roy Harris and Talbot J. Taylor, *Landmarks in Linguistic Thought*

symbols whose individual meanings cannot be deduced logically if you do not know anything else about them—Barthes looks at myths, or social norms, as human inventions rather than laws of nature. Barthes aims to critique society's tendency to behave as if these myths are eternal, unchangeable truths. The theorist Michel Foucault* also used semiotic analysis to criticize social structures: his work reveals how the norms and institutions in modern society have violent and repressive effects. Barthes and Foucault remain seminal figures in critical theory* and have a continuing impact on literary theory, philosophy, anthropology, and other fields. Through them, a version of Saussure's ideas can still be identified; for example, in radical twentieth and twenty-first century critiques of governments, unjust social institutions, and the consequences of the social and economic system of capitalism.*

Interaction

Saussure's model of the linguistic sign is placed in dialogue with that of the American philosopher and scientist Charles Sanders Peirce.* Saussure is known for his tripartite (three-part) chain of meaning— sign, signifier,* and signified,* where the sign and signifier are bound together—but Peirce developed a different concept of how signs work. For Peirce, everything was a sign, even human thought. Instead of seeing signs as something outside the mind that exist in the world, Peirce believed that signs are the building blocks of human thought. Peirce also developed a three-part process for analyzing signs: his system is composed of a sign (which he calls the "representatum"); an object (or "referent"); and the "interpretant." The sign is the same as Saussure's signifier: the word, sound, or symbol that indicates a thing or an idea. The "object" is whatever is represented by the sign. Lastly, the "interpretant" is the meaning conveyed by the representatum about the object, (the effect of the representatum on the person seeing or hearing it). Peirce calls the relationship between these three parts "semiosis."[2]

Peirce's semiotics* inspired the work of the Russian linguist Roman Jakobson* and the Italian literary theorist Umberto Eco* and their critiques of Saussure. Jakobson has made perhaps the most enduring critique of Saussure by arguing against the arbitrary nature of the sign and by citing Peirce to show that Saussure fails to explain fully the relationship between sign and signified—that is, how ideas translate between human thought and material reality.[3]

Studies of Saussure's thought show no sign of slowing down, with scholars such as John E. Joseph,* Roy Harris,* and Simon Bouquet* continuing to research into Saussure, his life, and semiotic theory. While these scholars' interpretations of Saussure's legacy differ, they are united in their focus on Saussure's life and social and historic context, in an attempt to assess his theories and their impact.

The Continuing Debate

Saussure's work is very important to two different academic disciplines: linguistics and semiotics. Saussure's name has become a byword for linguistic study, with the modern era being defined as "post-Saussurean."[4] Saussure's concept of the sign remains key to the study of both linguistics and semiotics. Regardless of the various criticisms of Saussure, his original idea that it is necessary to study the relationship between signs and society remains his most important legacy.

One of the most influential thinkers who took up Saussure's work outside of linguistics is the French anthropologist Claude Lévi-Strauss.* His application of structuralism* to the field of anthropology changed the discipline and created a new framework for studying indigenous cultures with his argument that the "civilized" mind has the same structure as the "savage" mind. He also approached kinship (family) relations as a system that could be analyzed with structural methods. His structuralist approach still dominates many anthropology departments in the United States and Europe.

In 1988, the US cultural critic Henry Louis Gates Jr.* wrote *The Signifying Monkey: A Theory of African-American Literary Criticism*. In this important work of cultural theory, Gates uses Saussure's categories of signifier and signified to analyze African American literature and vernacular speech—one example of how Saussure's structuralism continues to inform literary theory up until today. In addition to analyzing race as a system constructed by society, structuralism has also been used to think about gender. Judith Butler* of the United States, one of the most influential contemporary thinkers in feminism, uses structuralism and poststructuralism* as the springboard for her analysis of gender, sex, and power[5] ("feminism" here refers to the many intellectual and political currents relating to the struggle for equality between the sexes).

NOTES

1   Ferdinand de Saussure, *Course in General Linguistics*, ed. Perry Meisel and Haun Saussy, trans. Wade Baskin (New York: Columbia University Press, 2011), 16.

2   Saussure, *General Linguistics*, 42–3.

3   Roman Jakobson, "Sign and System of Language: A Reassessment of Saussure's Doctrine," in *Verbal Art, Verbal Sign, Verbal Time*, ed. Krystyna

Pomorska and Stephen Rudy (Minneapolis: Minnesota University Press, 1985), 30.

4   See Catherine Belsey, *Critical Practice* (London: Routledge, 2002) for a wider explanation of Saussureanism and post-Saussureanism.

5   See Judith Butler, *Gender Trouble* (London: Routledge, 2011). Butler's subsequent works build on her deconstruction of structures of gender and power.

WHERE NEXT?

KEY POINTS

- Saussure's *General Linguistics* will remain the definitive introduction to semiotics* for twenty-first century students and scholars.

- As language and technology change, Saussure's ideas can still be applied to understand how society communicates and understands itself.

- While there is still debate about Saussure's ideas, there is no doubt that Saussure fundamentally changed the field of linguistics* when he proposed that each individual language is a system of signs* that relate to each other more than to anything outside the system.

Potential

Ferdinand de Saussure's *Course in General Linguistics* is a seminal text in the fields of linguistics and semiotics. Its enduring appeal is partly a result of how broad and general it is. The text seeks to discuss languages at all times and in all places, and has applications beyond linguistics in the form of Saussure's concept of a general science of signs, out of which semiotics has developed. Saussure's theory has been applied to countless different studies and subject areas. The text was compiled and published from lecture notes by his pupils after Saussure's death and has always been unusually open to interpretation as a result. Some read the book as a nonhistorical approach to linguistics, while others understand the text as a general theory that can be applied to particular historical contexts, for example.

❝ For most innovative thinkers, there is little need to distinguish between the impact of their teaching and the influence of their writings as both have sprung from the same source and usually simultaneously ... In the case of Saussure, the situation is far more complex. ❞
Paul Bouissac, *Saussure: A Guide for the Perplexed*

Semiotics has reached beyond the linguistic framework first set by Saussure, and is used by theorists such as the influential French thinkers Roland Barthes,* Michel Foucault,* and Jacques Lacan.* The search for a clear definition of semiotics is difficult, because it is so widely used. In its most general sense, semiotics is the "science that studies the life of signs" that Saussure proposed[1]—the study of how meaning and communication work.

The literary theorist Winfried Nöth's* study of semiotics suggests that the science of signs will continue to evolve as society itself evolves.[2] Semiotics has been applied to many disciplines that did not even exist in Saussure's day, such as film studies or gender studies. Nöth contends that, because our sign systems are always changing and developing and because the science is relatively young, it is part of the nature of semiotics that its definition remains fluid.

Future Directions

Interpretations of Saussure's work are constantly evolving, and there has been continued interest in his concept of the sign system as the key method of communication in society. For example, the scholar Boris Gasparov* published a book in 2013 arguing that Saussure's epistemology*—that is, his system of knowing—was influenced by German Romanticism* and idealism.*[3] ("Romanticism" was a cultural movement at its peak in the nineteenth century and founded on a particular aesthetic of emotion and nature; "idealism" refers to a philosophical school holding that reality exists as a product of human thought rather than in and of itself.) This study places Saussure in the tradition of German Enlightenment thinking and opens up new possibilities for studying Saussure's thought in relation to continental philosophy. (The Enlightenment was a turn in eighteenth-century European culture towards rationality and liberty, and away from tradition and the influence of things such as religion.)

Saussure's theories are also used beyond the social sciences. Academics have even recently sought to apply Saussurean theories to mathematics and natural science.[4]

The scholars Perry Meisel* and Haun Saussy's* introduction to the latest English critical edition of *General Linguistics* (2011) emphasizes an approach to Saussure's work that draws on the aims and methods of many academic disciplines, suggesting that the enduring interest in Saussure stems from "how precise Saussure's solution is to a series of familiar, and presumably intractable, problems in the history of ideas"—problems that apply to many different disciplines. This implies that although Saussure's theory is open to interpretation, it is attractive because of its clarity.[5] Meisel and Saussy consider how the vast scholarship on Saussure has affected the text's impact on the arts and social sciences. For example, they outline the continuing debate in the fields of linguistics, cultural theory, and philosophy concerning questions of the sign's material nature (is it possible, for example, for a sign to be abstract or conceptual, or must it have a material quality in terms of sound or image?).

Summary

Modern linguistics can hardly be understood without Ferdinand de Saussure's *Course in General Linguistics*. The text identified a new direction for linguistic study by introducing the idea that all languages operate according to one general system. Saussure gave birth to linguistic structuralism*—the idea that all parts of a language should be understood as aspects of a unified system—and this revolutionized language study. Saussure's thought helped create the modern field of linguistics and would go on to influence other fields, such as literary theory, anthropology,* and philosophy of language. Saussure's discussion of the three-part linguistic sign (sign, signified,* and signifier)* has provoked debate since the publication of *General Linguistics*. Saussure indicated that his concept of the sign was applicable to many fields beyond linguistics, as it is central to the way in which human beings communicate and interact with the world. This idea evolved into the field of semiotics, which is important in a vast range of social sciences today; the idea that the sign is arbitrary, or not based on external rules, provided the framework for twentieth-century critiques of how society understands and maintains itself.

Perhaps the most curious aspect of Saussure's life and work is that he never published the ideas contained in the text during his lifetime; it was his former students who compiled the book from the notes they had made during his lectures. This is one reason why Saussure's work has fostered continuing interest more than 100 years after his original lectures. It has led to a mystique surrounding Saussure and an academic urge to discover the "real" Saussure—that is, to work out exactly which parts of the text were central to his thinking.

By reading *General Linguistics* in the present day through the lens of his many interpreters and alongside more recently published manuscripts and papers by Saussure, it can be understood freshly as the work of a scholar seeking to create a scientific method in the discipline of linguistics for others to use in analyzing specific languages and contexts.

NOTES

1   Ferdinand de Saussure, *Course in General Linguistics*, ed. Perry Meisel and Haun Saussy, trans. Wade Baskin (New York: Columbia University Press, 2011), 16.

2   Winfried Nöth, *Handbook of Semiotics* (Bloomington: Indiana University Press, 1990), 4–5.

3   Boris Gasparov, *Beyond Pure Reason: Ferdinand de Saussure's Philosophy of Language and Its Early Romantic Antecedents* (New York: Columbia University Press, 2013)

4   For example, see Paul Thibault, *Re-reading Saussure: The Dynamics of Signs in Social Life* (London: Routledge, 1997).

5   Perry Meisel and Haun Saussy, "Saussure and His Contexts," introduction to Saussure, *General Linguistics*, xx.

GLOSSARY

GLOSSARY OF TERMS

Ablaut: a form of change in vowels in the root of a word.

Anthropology: the study of human beings, commonly conducted through the analysis of societies and cultures.

Binary: composed of two elements.

Calvinism: a form of Protestant Christianity founded by John Calvin (1509–64), which stresses the importance of predestination (the idea that God has already decided who will be saved and who will be damned).

Capitalism: an economic system in which goods and services that are privately owned are sold or exchanged for profit.

Comparative linguistics: a method of linguistic study that compares different languages in order to work out the historical connections between them, categorizing languages into groups in order to understand patterns and changes in languages across times and places.

Critical theory: an approach to the analysis of society and culture commonly conducted on political lines and drawing on the theoretical innovations of the psychoanalyst Sigmund Freud and the political theorist Karl Marx.

Diachronic linguistics: the use of a historical, developmental approach to linguistic study.

Epistemology: system of knowledge.

Etymology: the history of the origin of words. Etymology also studies the history of words and their changes over time.

Genitive: a grammatical case in which a noun is changed by another noun.

Geneva school: a group of linguists, the most important of whom was Saussure, who were based around Geneva; other members included Albert Sechehaye, Albert Riedlinger, and Charles Bally.

Formalism: the theory that nature and the systems within it are determined by fixed or formal principles.

German Romanticism: an intellectual, literary, and artistic movement in eighteenth- and nineteenth-century Germany. One of the concerns of Romanticism was uncovering the true national spirit and preserving folk customs and language.

Hittite: an extinct language of present-day Syria and southern Turkey, spoken in the sixteenth to thirteenth centuries B.C.E.

Idealism: a trend in European philosophy holding that all of reality exists as a product of human thought rather than in and of itself. Idealism is interested in how subjectivity, thought, and perception create reality and not how things exist independent of the mind.

Indo-European: a family of several hundred related languages and dialects, including most major current languages of Europe, and parts of Western, Central and South Asia.

Knight of the French Legion of Honor: a special title granted by the French state for exceptional service or merit.

Langue: literally, "language" in French. In Saussure's system, *langue* refers to the system of language used by society independent from the individual.

Laryngeals: a postulated (that is, reconstructed or proposed) consonant that exists in Indo-European languages.

Linguistics: the scientific study of language and its structure. Modern linguists focus on how languages work at any given point in time, researching grammar and meaning, language, and the structure of communication.

Neogrammarian school: a group of nineteenth-century German linguists who believed that linguistic historical changes happen immediately rather than gradually.

Parole: in Saussure's system, *parole* (the French word for the English "speech") refers to everyday speech used by individuals. It is the result of individual ideas, action, and agency.

Philology: the study of language in written texts, commonly conducted with a view to improve understanding of the development of and relationships between languages.

Phonetic: concerned with speech sounds or spoken language; pronunciation.

Phonology: the study of the organization of sounds in language.

Psychoanalysis: a method of analyzing the mind by studying the subconscious through dreams, free association etc., founded and made famous by the Austrian neurologist Sigmund Freud.

Poststructuralism: a movement that began in the 1960s and 1970s, extending and challenging structuralism, suggesting that meanings are less stable and more open to interpretation than structuralism allows. Poststructuralism is associated with thinkers like Jacques Derrida and Roland Barthes.

Sanskrit: an ancient Indo-European language and the source for modern Hindi; Sanskrit was a popular field of study for linguists in the nineteenth century.

Semiology: Saussure's original term for the science of signs, the modern-day field of semiotics.

Semiotics: originally named "semiology" by Saussure, semiotics is the science of signs; the study of how humans communicate by means of systems of signs and symbols.

Sign: in Saussure's semiotic system, the sign is made up of the "signified" and the "signifier;" it is, in other words, the combination of a material signifier (an image or a printed word, for example) and a signified (the meaning it expresses).

Signified: what is referenced by the "signifier" (the physical presence of a sign, in sound or in text); for example, the signifier "tree" refers to the signified, a plant with a trunk, branches and leaves.

Signifier: the "sound-image" or the physical presence of a sign, in sound or in text. The signifier is always paired with the "signified" (the concept) to make a sign; for example, the signifier "tree" refers to the signified, a plant with a trunk, branches and leaves.

Sociology: the study of society and social behavior.

Structuralism: the theory that language is a system whose various parts only have meaning in relation to the system as a whole.

Structural linguistics: an approach to linguistics used by Saussure, in which empirical data is used to prove that all language functions by means of the same basic structure.

Synchronic linguistics: the use of a systematic, nonhistorical approach to linguistic study, analyzing data in a particular moment in time.

Syntax: the rules concerning such things as word order in a sentence.

World War II (1939–45): a large-scale military conflict that pitted the Axis powers—Germany, Italy, and Japan—against the Allies—Great Britain, France, the United States, and the Soviet Union.

PEOPLE MENTIONED IN THE TEXT

Mikhail Bakhtin (1895–1975) was a Russian literary theorist and author of numerous works including *Speech Genres and Other Late Essays* (1979). He argued that living languages must be studied alongside general linguistic theories.

Charles Bally (1865–1947) was a Swiss linguist from the Geneva School; one of Saussure's students, he edited Saussure's *Course in General Linguistics* for publication.

Dirk Baecker (b. 1955) is a German sociologist. His research follows the work of Niklas Luhmann and focuses on cultural theory and systems of communication in society.

Roland Barthes (1915–80) was a French literary critic and author. He is best known for his work on myth, images, photography, and the notion of the "death of the author" (the idea that texts should be studied separately from the life of the author).

Leonard Bloomfield (1887–1949) was an American linguist and structuralist. His is best known for his work in the 1930s and 1940s on structural linguistics and Native American languages.

Franz Bopp (1791–1867) was a German linguist and specialist in Indo-European languages. The author of *A Comparative Grammar* (1833), he conducted research into the connections between Sanskrit and European languages.

Simon Bouquet (b. 1954) is a lecturer in linguistics at Université Paris–Ouest Nanterre. He devotes his research to Saussure's manuscripts and edited a recent edition of Saussure's *Course in General Linguistics*.

Noam Chomsky (b. 1928) is an American linguist, philosopher, professor, and political activist. He is the author of many texts on linguistics and politics.

Jonathan Culler (b. 1944) is professor of English at Cornell University. He is the author of many works on literary theory.

Georg Curtius (1820–85) was a prominent German philologist. He is the author of *Comparative Philology in Its Relationship to Classical Philology* (1845).

Jacques Derrida (1930–2004) was a French literary theorist who spent much of his career in the United States. The author of *Of Grammatology* (1967), he elaborated the theory of "deconstruction," theorizing that language always has political meaning and exists in a hierarchy in which concepts compete for supremacy.

Umberto Eco (b. 1932) is an Italian author and scholar of semiotics and literature. He is the author of *Semiotics and the Philosophy of Language* (1984) and *The Name of the Rose* (1980), and has applied structuralist techniques to philosophy, art, film, literary criticism, and writing novels.

Rudolf Engler (1930–2003) was a lecturer in linguistics at the University of Bern. He specialized in Saussure studies and edited an edition of Saussure's *Course in General Linguistics*.

Michel Foucault (1926–84) was a French literary critic, social theorist, and philosopher. He was associated with both the structuralist and poststructuralist movements of the twentieth century.

Sigmund Freud (1856–1939) was an Austrian neurologist. Regarded as the founder of the therapeutic and theoretical approach to the unconscious mind known as psychoanalysis, Freud is considered to be one of the most influential scholars of the last century.

Boris Gasparov is Boris Bakhmeteff Professor of Russian and East European Studies at Columbia University.

Henry Louis Gates Jr. (b. 1950) is an American author, cultural critic, and historian. He is most known for his research and editorial work on race in America.

Jacob Grimm (1785–1863) was a German philologist and author. He is best known for writing collections of folktales with his brother Wilhelm, including *Grimm's Fairy Tales* (1812–22).

Roy Harris (1931–2015) was emeritus professor of Linguistics at the University of Oxford. He specialized in semiotics and Saussure studies and wrote a number of books on Saussure, including *Saussure and His Interpreters* (2001).

Louis Hjelmslev (1899–1965) was a Danish linguist and the founder of the Copenhagen school of structural linguists. He is the author of *Prolegomena to a Theory of Language* (1943), where he elaborated a four-part sign system in which both content and expression are important.

Roman Jakobson (1896–1982) was a Russian linguist and literary scholar. The author of "The Poetry of Grammar and the Grammar of Poetry" in *Selected Writings vol. III* (1981), he modified Saussurean sign theory and applied it to literary study.

John E. Joseph (b. 1956) is professor of applied linguistics at the University of Edinburgh, and the author of a biography of Saussure's life, which frames Saussure's work within contemporary socio-culture.

Eisuke Komatsu (b. 1940) is a Japanese linguist and professor. She has edited Saussure's notebooks and translated some of his works into Japanese.

Jacques Lacan (1901–81) was a French psychoanalyst who contributed to linguistics and critical theory. Lacan is known for bringing about a return to the study of Sigmund Freud and proposing new models for understanding psychological development and the role of desire in the human psyche.

August Leskien (1840–1916) was a Baltic and Slavic language specialist and central member of the Neogrammarian group of scholars. He established Leskien's Law, a sound law pertaining to Lithuanian vowels.

Claude Lévi-Strauss (1908–2009) was a French anthropologist. He is the author of *Myth and Meaning* (1978), in which he created structural theories of both the concepts of the family and the myth.

Niklas Luhmann (1927–98) was a German sociologist and social theorist who profoundly shaped the field of systems theory in the twentieth century. His many publications developed a theory of how communication functions in different systems, where the systems are different parts of society.

Antoine Meillet (1866–1936) was a French linguist. He was influenced by Saussure and took over Saussure's course on comparative linguistics in Geneva after Saussure stopped lecturing.

Perry Meisel (b. 1949) is professor of English at New York University, specializing in modern literature and critical theory. He is the author of *The Myth of the Modern: A Study in British Literature and Criticism after 1850* (1987), as well as works on Saussure.

Winfried Nöth (b. 1944) is professor of English linguistics at Kassel University, Germany, specializing in semiotics. He is the author of multiple books on semiotics and literary texts.

Charles Sanders Peirce (1839–1914) was known as the "father of pragmatism." The author of "What is a Sign?" (1894), he theorized a tripartite (three-part) sign, similar to that of Saussure's, in the early twentieth century.

Albert Riedlinger was a student of Saussure's, and collaborated with Charles Bally and Albert Sechehaye on the publication of *Course in General Linguistics.*

Henri Louis Frédéric de Saussure (1829–1905) was a Swiss mineralogist and taxidermist. He was the father of Ferdinand de Saussure.

Horace-Bénédict de Saussure (1740–99) was a Swiss chemist and alpinist. He conducted important research on solar power and mineral studies.

Carol Sanders is a linguist and professor emerita of the University of Surrey. Her academic work focuses on the history of linguistics, structuralism, and the legacy of Saussure.

Haun Saussy (b. 1960) is professor of comparative literature at the University of Chicago, with a particular interest in Chinese Literature.

He is the author of *The Problem of a Chinese Aesthetic* (1993) and works on Saussure.

August Schleicher (1821–68) was a German linguist. He is the author of *A Compendium of the Comparative Grammar of the Indo-European, Sansktrit, Greek and Latin Languages* (1874), which sought to prove that all Indo-European languages came from a common root by reconstructing a proto-Indo-European language.

Albert Sechehaye (1870–1946) was a Swiss linguist and student of Saussure. He was one of the editors of the *Course in General Linguistics*.

Nikolai Trubetskoy (1890–1938) was a linguist and member of the Prague School of Linguistics, noted for his work in phonology and membership of the Eurasianist movement.

Valentin Vološinov (1895–1936) was a Russian linguist. He is the author of *Marxism and the Philosophy of Language* (1929), which fuses Saussure's conception of language as a sign system with the idea that language is constantly being created dynamically in social contexts.

William Dwight Whitney (1827–94) was a prominent American linguist and founder of the American Philological Association. He is the author of *The Life and Growth of Language: An Outline of Linguistic Science* (1875).

Ernst Windisch (1844–1918) was a well-known German linguist who specialized in Indo-European languages. He is the author of *Compendium of Irish Grammar* (1883).

WORKS CITED

WORKS CITED

Baecker, Dirk, ed. Translated by Michael Irmscher and Leah Edwards. *Problems of Form.* Stanford, CA: Stanford University Press, 1999.

Belsey, Catherine. *Critical Practice.* London: Routledge, 2002.

Bouissac, Paul. *Saussure: A Guide for the Perplexed.* New York: Continuum, 2010.

Culler, Jonathan. *Ferdinand de Saussure.* New York: Penguin Books, 1977.

Eco, Umberto. *Foucault's Pendulum.* Translated by William Weaver. London: Picador, 1990.

— — —. *The Name of the Rose.* Translated by William Weaver. New York and London: Everyman's Library, 2006.

Harris, Roy. *Saussure and His Interpreters*. Edinburgh: Edinburgh University Press, 2003.

Harris, Roy, and Talbot J. Taylor. *Landmarks in Linguistic Thought I: The Western Tradition from Socrates to Saussure.* London: Routledge, 1997.

Joseph, John E. *Saussure.* Oxford: Oxford University Press, 2012.

Krampen, Martin. "Ferdinand de Saussure and the Development of Semiology." In *Classics of Semiotics*, ed. Martin Krampen et al, 66–77. New York: Plenum Press, 1987.

Luhmann, Niklas. "'Sign as Form'—A Comment." *Cybernetics and Human Knowing* 6, no.3 (1999): 39–46.

Nöth, Winfried. *Handbook of Semiotics.* Bloomington, IN: Indiana University Press, 1990.

Sanders, Carol, ed. *The Cambridge Companion to Saussure.* Cambridge: Cambridge University Press, 2004.

Saussure, Ferdinand de. *Course in General Linguistics.* Edited by Charles Bally and Albert Sechehaye, with Albert Riedlinger. Translated by Wade Baskin. London: Peter Owen, 1959.

— — —. *Course in General Linguistics.* Edited by Charles Bally and Albert Sechehaye, with Albert Riedlinger. Translated by Roy Harris. London: Duckworth, 1983.

— — —. *Course in General Linguistics*. Edited by Perry Meisel and Haun Saussy. Translated by Wade Baskin. New York: Columbia University Press, 2011.

————. *Mémoire sur le Système Primitif des Voyelles dans les Langues Indo-Européennes*. Leipzig: B. G. Teubner, 1879.

————. *Writings in General Linguistics*. Edited by Simon Bouquet and Rudolf Engler. Translated by Carol Sanders and Matthew Pires. Oxford: Oxford University Press, 2006.

Thibault, Paul. *Re-reading Saussure: The Dynamics of Signs in Social Life.* London: Routledge, 1997.

Whitney, William Dwight. *The Life and Growth of Language: An Outline of Linguistic Science*. New York: Dover, 1979.

THE MACAT LIBRARY
BY DISCIPLINE

AFRICANA STUDIES

Chinua Achebe's *An Image of Africa: Racism in Conrad's Heart of Darkness*
W. E. B. Du Bois's *The Souls of Black Folk*
Zora Neale Huston's *Characteristics of Negro Expression*
Martin Luther King Jr's *Why We Can't Wait*
Toni Morrison's *Playing in the Dark: Whiteness in the American Literary Imagination*

ANTHROPOLOGY

Arjun Appadurai's *Modernity at Large: Cultural Dimensions of Globalisation*
Philippe Ariès's *Centuries of Childhood*
Franz Boas's *Race, Language and Culture*
Kim Chan & Renée Mauborgne's *Blue Ocean Strategy*
Jared Diamond's *Guns, Germs & Steel: the Fate of Human Societies*
Jared Diamond's *Collapse: How Societies Choose to Fail or Survive*
E. E. Evans-Pritchard's *Witchcraft, Oracles and Magic Among the Azande*
James Ferguson's *The Anti-Politics Machine*
Clifford Geertz's *The Interpretation of Cultures*
David Graeber's *Debt: the First 5000 Years*
Karen Ho's *Liquidated: An Ethnography of Wall Street*
Geert Hofstede's *Culture's Consequences: Comparing Values, Behaviors, Institutes and Organizations across Nations*
Claude Lévi-Strauss's *Structural Anthropology*
Jay Macleod's *Ain't No Makin' It: Aspirations and Attainment in a Low-Income Neighborhood*
Saba Mahmood's *The Politics of Piety: The Islamic Revival and the Feminist Subject*
Marcel Mauss's *The Gift*

BUSINESS

Jean Lave & Etienne Wenger's *Situated Learning*
Theodore Levitt's *Marketing Myopia*
Burton G. Malkiel's *A Random Walk Down Wall Street*
Douglas McGregor's *The Human Side of Enterprise*
Michael Porter's *Competitive Strategy: Creating and Sustaining Superior Performance*
John Kotter's *Leading Change*
C. K. Prahalad & Gary Hamel's *The Core Competence of the Corporation*

CRIMINOLOGY

Michelle Alexander's *The New Jim Crow: Mass Incarceration in the Age of Colorblindness*
Michael R. Gottfredson & Travis Hirschi's *A General Theory of Crime*
Richard Herrnstein & Charles A. Murray's *The Bell Curve: Intelligence and Class Structure in American Life*
Elizabeth Loftus's *Eyewitness Testimony*
Jay Macleod's *Ain't No Makin' It: Aspirations and Attainment in a Low-Income Neighborhood*
Philip Zimbardo's *The Lucifer Effect*

ECONOMICS

Janet Abu-Lughod's *Before European Hegemony*
Ha-Joon Chang's *Kicking Away the Ladder*
David Brion Davis's *The Problem of Slavery in the Age of Revolution*
Milton Friedman's *The Role of Monetary Policy*
Milton Friedman's *Capitalism and Freedom*
David Graeber's *Debt: the First 5000 Years*
Friedrich Hayek's *The Road to Serfdom*
Karen Ho's *Liquidated: An Ethnography of Wall Street*

John Maynard Keynes's *The General Theory of Employment, Interest and Money*
Charles P. Kindleberger's *Manias, Panics and Crashes*
Robert Lucas's *Why Doesn't Capital Flow from Rich to Poor Countries?*
Burton G. Malkiel's *A Random Walk Down Wall Street*
Thomas Robert Malthus's *An Essay on the Principle of Population*
Karl Marx's *Capital*
Thomas Piketty's *Capital in the Twenty-First Century*
Amartya Sen's *Development as Freedom*
Adam Smith's *The Wealth of Nations*
Nassim Nicholas Taleb's *The Black Swan: The Impact of the Highly Improbable*
Amos Tversky's & Daniel Kahneman's *Judgment under Uncertainty: Heuristics and Biases*
Mahbub Ul Haq's *Reflections on Human Development*
Max Weber's *The Protestant Ethic and the Spirit of Capitalism*

FEMINISM AND GENDER STUDIES

Judith Butler's *Gender Trouble*
Simone De Beauvoir's *The Second Sex*
Michel Foucault's *History of Sexuality*
Betty Friedan's *The Feminine Mystique*
Saba Mahmood's *The Politics of Piety: The Islamic Revival and the Feminist Subjec*t
Joan Wallach Scott's *Gender and the Politics of History*
Mary Wollstonecraft's *A Vindication of the Rights of Woman*
Virginia Woolf's *A Room of One's Own*

GEOGRAPHY

The Brundtland Report's *Our Common Future*
Rachel Carson's *Silent Spring*
Charles Darwin's *On the Origin of Species*
James Ferguson's *The Anti-Politics Machine*
Jane Jacobs's *The Death and Life of Great American Cities*
James Lovelock's *Gaia: A New Look at Life on Earth*
Amartya Sen's *Development as Freedom*
Mathis Wackernagel & William Rees's *Our Ecological Footprint*

HISTORY

Janet Abu-Lughod's *Before European Hegemony*
Benedict Anderson's *Imagined Communities*
Bernard Bailyn's *The Ideological Origins of the American Revolution*
Hanna Batatu's *The Old Social Classes And The Revolutionary Movements Of Iraq*
Christopher Browning's *Ordinary Men: Reserve Police Batallion 101 and the Final Solution in Poland*
Edmund Burke's *Reflections on the Revolution in France*
William Cronon's *Nature's Metropolis: Chicago And The Great West*
Alfred W. Crosby's *The Columbian Exchange*
Hamid Dabashi's *Iran: A People Interrupted*
David Brion Davis's *The Problem of Slavery in the Age of Revolution*
Nathalie Zemon Davis's *The Return of Martin Guerre*
Jared Diamond's *Guns, Germs & Steel: the Fate of Human Societies*
Frank Dikotter's *Mao's Great Famine*
John W Dower's *War Without Mercy: Race And Power In The Pacific War*
W. E. B. Du Bois's *The Souls of Black Folk*
Richard J. Evans's *In Defence of History*
Lucien Febvre's *The Problem of Unbelief in the 16th Century*
Sheila Fitzpatrick's *Everyday Stalinism*

Eric Foner's *Reconstruction: America's Unfinished Revolution, 1863-1877*
Michel Foucault's *Discipline and Punish*
Michel Foucault's *History of Sexuality*
Francis Fukuyama's *The End of History and the Last Man*
John Lewis Gaddis's *We Now Know: Rethinking Cold War History*
Ernest Gellner's *Nations and Nationalism*
Eugene Genovese's *Roll, Jordan, Roll: The World the Slaves Made*
Carlo Ginzburg's *The Night Battles*
Daniel Goldhagen's *Hitler's Willing Executioners*
Jack Goldstone's *Revolution and Rebellion in the Early Modern World*
Antonio Gramsci's *The Prison Notebooks*
Alexander Hamilton, John Jay & James Madison's *The Federalist Papers*
Christopher Hill's *The World Turned Upside Down*
Carole Hillenbrand's *The Crusades: Islamic Perspectives*
Thomas Hobbes's *Leviathan*
Eric Hobsbawm's *The Age Of Revolution*
John A. Hobson's *Imperialism: A Study*
Albert Hourani's *History of the Arab Peoples*
Samuel P. Huntington's *The Clash of Civilizations and the Remaking of World Order*
C. L. R. James's *The Black Jacobins*
Tony Judt's *Postwar: A History of Europe Since 1945*
Ernst Kantorowicz's *The King's Two Bodies: A Study in Medieval Political Theology*
Paul Kennedy's *The Rise and Fall of the Great Powers*
Ian Kershaw's *The "Hitler Myth": Image and Reality in the Third Reich*
John Maynard Keynes's *The General Theory of Employment, Interest and Money*
Charles P. Kindleberger's *Manias, Panics and Crashes*
Martin Luther King Jr's *Why We Can't Wait*
Henry Kissinger's *World Order: Reflections on the Character of Nations and the Course of History*
Thomas Kuhn's *The Structure of Scientific Revolutions*
Georges Lefebvre's *The Coming of the French Revolution*
John Locke's *Two Treatises of Government*
Niccolò Machiavelli's *The Prince*
Thomas Robert Malthus's *An Essay on the Principle of Population*
Mahmood Mamdani's *Citizen and Subject: Contemporary Africa And The Legacy Of Late Colonialism*
Karl Marx's *Capital*
Stanley Milgram's *Obedience to Authority*
John Stuart Mill's *On Liberty*
Thomas Paine's *Common Sense*
Thomas Paine's *Rights of Man*
Geoffrey Parker's *Global Crisis: War, Climate Change and Catastrophe in the Seventeenth Century*
Jonathan Riley-Smith's *The First Crusade and the Idea of Crusading*
Jean-Jacques Rousseau's *The Social Contract*
Joan Wallach Scott's *Gender and the Politics of History*
Theda Skocpol's *States and Social Revolutions*
Adam Smith's *The Wealth of Nations*
Timothy Snyder's *Bloodlands: Europe Between Hitler and Stalin*
Sun Tzu's *The Art of War*
Keith Thomas's *Religion and the Decline of Magic*
Thucydides's *The History of the Peloponnesian War*
Frederick Jackson Turner's *The Significance of the Frontier in American History*
Odd Arne Westad's *The Global Cold War: Third World Interventions And The Making Of Our Times*

LITERATURE

Chinua Achebe's *An Image of Africa: Racism in Conrad's Heart of Darkness*
Roland Barthes's *Mythologies*
Homi K. Bhabha's *The Location of Culture*
Judith Butler's *Gender Trouble*
Simone De Beauvoir's *The Second Sex*
Ferdinand De Saussure's *Course in General Linguistics*
T. S. Eliot's *The Sacred Wood: Essays on Poetry and Criticism*
Zora Neale Huston's *Characteristics of Negro Expression*
Toni Morrison's *Playing in the Dark: Whiteness in the American Literary Imagination*
Edward Said's *Orientalism*
Gayatri Chakravorty Spivak's *Can the Subaltern Speak?*
Mary Wollstonecraft's *A Vindication of the Rights of Women*
Virginia Woolf's *A Room of One's Own*

PHILOSOPHY

Elizabeth Anscombe's *Modern Moral Philosophy*
Hannah Arendt's *The Human Condition*
Aristotle's *Metaphysics*
Aristotle's *Nicomachean Ethics*
Edmund Gettier's *Is Justified True Belief Knowledge?*
Georg Wilhelm Friedrich Hegel's *Phenomenology of Spirit*
David Hume's *Dialogues Concerning Natural Religion*
David Hume's *The Enquiry for Human Understanding*
Immanuel Kant's *Religion within the Boundaries of Mere Reason*
Immanuel Kant's *Critique of Pure Reason*
Søren Kierkegaard's *The Sickness Unto Death*
Søren Kierkegaard's *Fear and Trembling*
C. S. Lewis's *The Abolition of Man*
Alasdair MacIntyre's *After Virtue*
Marcus Aurelius's *Meditations*
Friedrich Nietzsche's *On the Genealogy of Morality*
Friedrich Nietzsche's *Beyond Good and Evil*
Plato's *Republic*
Plato's *Symposium*
Jean-Jacques Rousseau's *The Social Contract*
Gilbert Ryle's *The Concept of Mind*
Baruch Spinoza's *Ethics*
Sun Tzu's *The Art of War*
Ludwig Wittgenstein's *Philosophical Investigations*

POLITICS

Benedict Anderson's *Imagined Communities*
Aristotle's *Politics*
Bernard Bailyn's *The Ideological Origins of the American Revolution*
Edmund Burke's *Reflections on the Revolution in France*
John C. Calhoun's *A Disquisition on Government*
Ha-Joon Chang's *Kicking Away the Ladder*
Hamid Dabashi's *Iran: A People Interrupted*
Hamid Dabashi's *Theology of Discontent: The Ideological Foundation of the Islamic Revolution in Iran*
Robert Dahl's *Democracy and its Critics*
Robert Dahl's *Who Governs?*
David Brion Davis's *The Problem of Slavery in the Age of Revolution*

Alexis De Tocqueville's *Democracy in America*
James Ferguson's *The Anti-Politics Machine*
Frank Dikotter's *Mao's Great Famine*
Sheila Fitzpatrick's *Everyday Stalinism*
Eric Foner's *Reconstruction: America's Unfinished Revolution, 1863-1877*
Milton Friedman's *Capitalism and Freedom*
Francis Fukuyama's *The End of History and the Last Man*
John Lewis Gaddis's *We Now Know: Rethinking Cold War History*
Ernest Gellner's *Nations and Nationalism*
David Graeber's *Debt: the First 5000 Years*
Antonio Gramsci's *The Prison Notebooks*
Alexander Hamilton, John Jay & James Madison's *The Federalist Papers*
Friedrich Hayek's *The Road to Serfdom*
Christopher Hill's *The World Turned Upside Down*
Thomas Hobbes's *Leviathan*
John A. Hobson's *Imperialism: A Study*
Samuel P. Huntington's *The Clash of Civilizations and the Remaking of World Order*
Tony Judt's *Postwar: A History of Europe Since 1945*
David C. Kang's *China Rising: Peace, Power and Order in East Asia*
Paul Kennedy's *The Rise and Fall of Great Powers*
Robert Keohane's *After Hegemony*
Martin Luther King Jr.'s *Why We Can't Wait*
Henry Kissinger's *World Order: Reflections on the Character of Nations and the Course of History*
John Locke's *Two Treatises of Government*
Niccolò Machiavelli's *The Prince*
Thomas Robert Malthus's *An Essay on the Principle of Population*
Mahmood Mamdani's *Citizen and Subject: Contemporary Africa And The Legacy Of Late Colonialism*
Karl Marx's *Capital*
John Stuart Mill's *On Liberty*
John Stuart Mill's *Utilitarianism*
Hans Morgenthau's *Politics Among Nations*
Thomas Paine's *Common Sense*
Thomas Paine's *Rights of Man*
Thomas Piketty's *Capital in the Twenty-First Century*
Robert D. Putman's *Bowling Alone*
John Rawls's *Theory of Justice*
Jean-Jacques Rousseau's *The Social Contract*
Theda Skocpol's *States and Social Revolutions*
Adam Smith's *The Wealth of Nations*
Sun Tzu's *The Art of War*
Henry David Thoreau's *Civil Disobedience*
Thucydides's *The History of the Peloponnesian War*
Kenneth Waltz's *Theory of International Politics*
Max Weber's *Politics as a Vocation*
Odd Arne Westad's *The Global Cold War: Third World Interventions And The Making Of Our Times*

POSTCOLONIAL STUDIES

Roland Barthes's *Mythologies*
Frantz Fanon's *Black Skin, White Masks*
Homi K. Bhabha's *The Location of Culture*
Gustavo Gutiérrez's *A Theology of Liberation*
Edward Said's *Orientalism*
Gayatri Chakravorty Spivak's *Can the Subaltern Speak?*

PSYCHOLOGY

Gordon Allport's *The Nature of Prejudice*
Alan Baddeley & Graham Hitch's *Aggression: A Social Learning Analysis*
Albert Bandura's *Aggression: A Social Learning Analysis*
Leon Festinger's *A Theory of Cognitive Dissonance*
Sigmund Freud's *The Interpretation of Dreams*
Betty Friedan's *The Feminine Mystique*
Michael R. Gottfredson & Travis Hirschi's *A General Theory of Crime*
Eric Hoffer's *The True Believer: Thoughts on the Nature of Mass Movements*
William James's *Principles of Psychology*
Elizabeth Loftus's *Eyewitness Testimony*
A. H. Maslow's *A Theory of Human Motivation*
Stanley Milgram's *Obedience to Authority*
Steven Pinker's *The Better Angels of Our Nature*
Oliver Sacks's *The Man Who Mistook His Wife For a Hat*
Richard Thaler & Cass Sunstein's *Nudge: Improving Decisions About Health, Wealth and Happiness*
Amos Tversky's *Judgment under Uncertainty: Heuristics and Biases*
Philip Zimbardo's *The Lucifer Effect*

SCIENCE

Rachel Carson's *Silent Spring*
William Cronon's *Nature's Metropolis: Chicago And The Great West*
Alfred W. Crosby's *The Columbian Exchange*
Charles Darwin's *On the Origin of Species*
Richard Dawkin's *The Selfish Gene*
Thomas Kuhn's *The Structure of Scientific Revolutions*
Geoffrey Parker's *Global Crisis: War, Climate Change and Catastrophe in the Seventeenth Century*
Mathis Wackernagel & William Rees's *Our Ecological Footprint*

SOCIOLOGY

Michelle Alexander's *The New Jim Crow: Mass Incarceration in the Age of Colorblindness*
Gordon Allport's *The Nature of Prejudice*
Albert Bandura's *Aggression: A Social Learning Analysis*
Hanna Batatu's *The Old Social Classes And The Revolutionary Movements Of Iraq*
Ha-Joon Chang's *Kicking Away the Ladder*
W. E. B. Du Bois's *The Souls of Black Folk*
Émile Durkheim's *On Suicide*
Frantz Fanon's *Black Skin, White Masks*
Frantz Fanon's *The Wretched of the Earth*
Eric Foner's *Reconstruction: America's Unfinished Revolution, 1863-1877*
Eugene Genovese's *Roll, Jordan, Roll: The World the Slaves Made*
Jack Goldstone's *Revolution and Rebellion in the Early Modern World*
Antonio Gramsci's *The Prison Notebooks*
Richard Herrnstein & Charles A Murray's *The Bell Curve: Intelligence and Class Structure in American Life*
Eric Hoffer's *The True Believer: Thoughts on the Nature of Mass Movements*
Jane Jacobs's *The Death and Life of Great American Cities*
Robert Lucas's *Why Doesn't Capital Flow from Rich to Poor Countries?*
Jay Macleod's *Ain't No Makin' It: Aspirations and Attainment in a Low Income Neighborhood*
Elaine May's *Homeward Bound: American Families in the Cold War Era*
Douglas McGregor's *The Human Side of Enterprise*
C. Wright Mills's *The Sociological Imagination*

Thomas Piketty's *Capital in the Twenty-First Century*
Robert D. Putman's *Bowling Alone*
David Riesman's *The Lonely Crowd: A Study of the Changing American Character*
Edward Said's *Orientalism*
Joan Wallach Scott's *Gender and the Politics of History*
Theda Skocpol's *States and Social Revolutions*
Max Weber's *The Protestant Ethic and the Spirit of Capitalism*

THEOLOGY

Augustine's *Confessions*
Benedict's *Rule of St Benedict*
Gustavo Gutiérrez's *A Theology of Liberation*
Carole Hillenbrand's *The Crusades: Islamic Perspectives*
David Hume's *Dialogues Concerning Natural Religion*
Immanuel Kant's *Religion within the Boundaries of Mere Reason*
Ernst Kantorowicz's *The King's Two Bodies: A Study in Medieval Political Theology*
Søren Kierkegaard's *The Sickness Unto Death*
C. S. Lewis's *The Abolition of Man*
Saba Mahmood's *The Politics of Piety: The Islamic Revival and the Feminist Subject*
Baruch Spinoza's *Ethics*
Keith Thomas's *Religion and the Decline of Magic*

COMING SOON

Chris Argyris's *The Individual and the Organisation*
Seyla Benhabib's *The Rights of Others*
Walter Benjamin's *The Work Of Art in the Age of Mechanical Reproduction*
John Berger's *Ways of Seeing*
Pierre Bourdieu's *Outline of a Theory of Practice*
Mary Douglas's *Purity and Danger*
Roland Dworkin's *Taking Rights Seriously*
James G. March's *Exploration and Exploitation in Organisational Learning*
Ikujiro Nonaka's *A Dynamic Theory of Organizational Knowledge Creation*
Griselda Pollock's *Vision and Difference*
Amartya Sen's *Inequality Re-Examined*
Susan Sontag's *On Photography*
Yasser Tabbaa's *The Transformation of Islamic Art*
Ludwig von Mises's *Theory of Money and Credit*

The Macat Library By Discipline

Macat Disciplines

Access the greatest ideas and thinkers across entire disciplines, including

AFRICANA STUDIES

Chinua Achebe's *An Image of Africa: Racism in Conrad's Heart of Darkness*

W. E. B. Du Bois's *The Souls of Black Folk*

Zora Neale Hurston's *Characteristics of Negro Expression*

Martin Luther King Jr.'s *Why We Can't Wait*

Toni Morrison's *Playing in the Dark: Whiteness in the American Literary Imagination*

Macat analyses are available from all good bookshops and libraries.

Access hundreds of analyses through one, multimedia tool.
Join free for one month **library.macat.com**

Macat Disciplines

Access the greatest ideas and thinkers across entire disciplines, including

FEMINISM, GENDER AND QUEER STUDIES

Simone De Beauvoir's
The Second Sex

Michel Foucault's
History of Sexuality

Betty Friedan's
The Feminine Mystique

Saba Mahmood's
*The Politics of Piety:
The Islamic Revival and
the Feminist Subject*

Joan Wallach Scott's
*Gender and the
Politics of History*

Mary Wollstonecraft's
*A Vindication of the
Rights of Woman*

Virginia Woolf's
A Room of One's Own

Judith Butler's
Gender Trouble

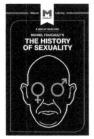

Macat analyses are available from all good bookshops and libraries.

Access hundreds of analyses through one, multimedia tool.
Join free for one month **library.macat.com**

Macat Disciplines

Access the greatest ideas and thinkers across entire disciplines, including

INEQUALITY

Ha-Joon Chang's, *Kicking Away the Ladder*

David Graeber's, *Debt: The First 5000 Years*

Robert E. Lucas's, *Why Doesn't Capital Flow from Rich To Poor Countries?*

Thomas Piketty's, *Capital in the Twenty-First Century*

Amartya Sen's, *Inequality Re-Examined*

Mahbub Ul Haq's, *Reflections on Human Development*

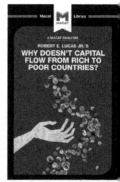

Macat analyses are available from all good bookshops and libraries.

Access hundreds of analyses through one, multimedia tool.
Join free for one month **library.macat.com**

Macat Disciplines

Access the greatest ideas and thinkers across entire disciplines, including

CRIMINOLOGY

Michelle Alexander's
The New Jim Crow: Mass Incarceration in the Age of Colorblindness

Michael R. Gottfredson & Travis Hirschi's
A General Theory of Crime

Elizabeth Loftus's
Eyewitness Testimony

Richard Herrnstein & Charles A. Murray's
The Bell Curve: Intelligence and Class Structure in American Life

Jay Macleod's
Ain't No Makin' It: Aspirations and Attainment in a Low-Income Neighborhood

Philip Zimbardo's
The Lucifer Effect

Macat Disciplines

Access the greatest ideas and thinkers across entire disciplines, including

Postcolonial Studies

Roland Barthes's *Mythologies*
Frantz Fanon's *Black Skin, White Masks*
Homi K. Bhabha's *The Location of Culture*
Gustavo Gutiérrez's *A Theology of Liberation*
Edward Said's *Orientalism*
Gayatri Chakravorty Spivak's *Can the Subaltern Speak?*

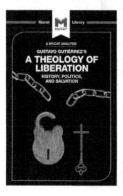

Macat Disciplines

Access the greatest ideas and thinkers across entire disciplines, including

GLOBALIZATION

Arjun Appadurai's, *Modernity at Large: Cultural Dimensions of Globalisation*

James Ferguson's, *The Anti-Politics Machine*

Geert Hofstede's, *Culture's Consequences*

Amartya Sen's, *Development as Freedom*

Macat Pairs

Analyse historical and modern issues from opposite sides of an argument. Pairs include:

MACAT

MACAT

HOW TO RUN AN ECONOMY

John Maynard Keynes's
The General Theory OF Employment, Interest and Money

Classical economics suggests that market economies are self-correcting in times of recession or depression, and tend toward full employment and output. But English economist John Maynard Keynes disagrees.

In his ground-breaking 1936 study *The General Theory*, Keynes argues that traditional economics has misunderstood the causes of unemployment. Employment is not determined by the price of labor; it is directly linked to demand. Keynes believes market economies are by nature unstable, and so require government intervention. Spurred on by the social catastrophe of the Great Depression of the 1930s, he sets out to revolutionize the way the world thinks

Milton Friedman's
The Role of Monetary Policy

Friedman's 1968 paper changed the course of economic theory. In just 17 pages, he demolished existing theory and outlined an effective alternate monetary policy designed to secure 'high employment stable prices and rapid growth.'

Friedman demonstrated that monetary policy plays a vital role in broader economic stability and argued that economists got their monetary policy wrong in the 1950s and 1960s by misunderstanding the relationship between inflation and unemployment. Previous generations of economists had believed that governments could permanently decrease unemployment by permitting inflation—and vice versa Friedman's most original contribution was to show that this supposed trade-off is an illusion that only works in the short term.

Macat analyses are available from all good bookshops and libraries.

Access hundreds of analyses through one, multimedia tool.
Join free for one month **library.macat.com**

Macat Disciplines

Access the greatest ideas and thinkers across entire disciplines, including

THE FUTURE OF DEMOCRACY

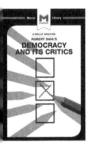

Robert A. Dahl's, *Democracy and Its Critics*
Robert A. Dahl's, *Who Governs?*
Alexis De Toqueville's, *Democracy in America*
Niccolò Machiavelli's, *The Prince*
John Stuart Mill's, *On Liberty*
Robert D. Putnam's, *Bowling Alone*
Jean-Jacques Rousseau's, *The Social Contract*
Henry David Thoreau's, *Civil Disobedience*

Macat Disciplines

Access the greatest ideas and thinkers across entire disciplines, including

TOTALITARIANISM

Sheila Fitzpatrick's, *Everyday Stalinism*
Ian Kershaw's, *The "Hitler Myth"*
Timothy Snyder's, *Bloodlands*

Macat Pairs

Analyse historical and modern issues from opposite sides of an argument. Pairs include:

RACE AND IDENTITY

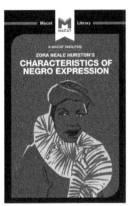

Zora Neale Hurston's
Characteristics of Negro Expression

Using material collected on anthropological expeditions to the South, Zora Neale Hurston explains how expression in African American culture in the early twentieth century departs from the art of white America. At the time, African American art was often criticized for copying white culture. For Hurston, this criticism misunderstood how art works. European tradition views art as something fixed. But Hurston describes a creative process that is alive, ever-changing, and largely improvisational. She maintains that African American art works through a process called 'mimicry'—where an imitated object or verbal pattern, for example, is reshaped and altered until it becomes something new, novel—and worthy of attention.

Frantz Fanon's
Black Skin, White Masks

Black Skin, White Masks offers a radical analysis of the psychological effects of colonization on the colonized.

Fanon witnessed the effects of colonization first hand both in his birthplace, Martinique, and again later in life when he worked as a psychiatrist in another French colony, Algeria. His text is uncompromising in form and argument. He dissects the dehumanizing effects of colonialism, arguing that it destroys the native sense of identity, forcing people to adapt to an alien set of values—including a core belief that they are inferior. This results in deep psychological trauma.

Fanon's work played a pivotal role in the civil rights movements of the 1960s.

Macat analyses are available from all good bookshops and libraries.

Access hundreds of analyses through one, multimedia tool.
Join free for one month **library.macat.com**

Macat Pairs

Analyse historical and modern issues from opposite sides of an argument. Pairs include:

INTERNATIONAL RELATIONS IN THE 21ST CENTURY

Samuel P. Huntington's
The Clash of Civilisations

In his highly influential 1996 book, Huntington offers a vision of a post-Cold War world in which conflict takes place not between competing ideologies but between cultures. The worst clash, he argues, will be between the Islamic world and the West: the West's arrogance and belief that its culture is a "gift" to the world will come into conflict with Islam's obstinacy and concern that its culture is under attack from a morally decadent "other."

Clash inspired much debate between different political schools of thought. But its greatest impact came in helping define American foreign policy in the wake of the 2001 terrorist attacks in New York and Washington.

Francis Fukuyama's
The End of History and the Last Man

Published in 1992, *The End of History and the Last Man* argues that capitalist democracy is the final destination for all societies. Fukuyama believed democracy triumphed during the Cold War because it lacks the "fundamental contradictions" inherent in communism and satisfies our yearning for freedom and equality. Democracy therefore marks the endpoint in the evolution of ideology, and so the "end of history." There will still be "events," but no fundamental change in ideology.

Printed in the United States
by Baker & Taylor Publisher Services